-profile entertainment legal cases and saw first-hand
special inside knowledge. His clients come out on top.
an all-around great guy.

that Rob and I did together, I thought I knew all about
w. But, when he asked me to read the first draft of his
m, I was stunned to discover how little I actually knew
children in entertainment. You can take my word that
help keep you in the know, and help you and your fam-
career-breaking mistakes."

**—Darryl O. Dickey, Attorney at Law**

ed with me on several cases and contracts, and I have to
a way of removing all the burden from the legal process,
t in a manner that is lucid and concise. He's always pro-
lear explanations so I may be able to fully consider my
advice is consistently spot-on. In all my years working
yers in the Entertainment field, he's not only the most
I've come across; he also has some really good instincts,
d one that's been instrumental to my various successes.
ly not least, he cares."

**—Audrey Martinez, Actress/Model/Film Producer**

li is an excellent attorney and a very likable person. He's
wledgeable about Entertainment Law, especially with
t Agents and contracts dealing with minors. I had the
rking with Mr. Pafundi on several successful entertain-
nd have benefited from his insight and mentoring."

**th Robinson, Attorney at Law, Los Angeles, California**

obert Pafundi for over 30 years as a friend and an associ-
as an attorney are top-notch, and more importantly, he is
highest integrity. He is highly respected by his clients for
honesty, and I've seen the respect he receives from his
well. As an Entertainment Law attorney and dad, he truly
nd cares for children and their families."

**—Gary L. Schank, Attorney at Law**

# 1

"Having worked with Ro
and contract negotiation
less than great quality. H
and always puts in the ti
addition, he has many yea
him the expertise in litiga
actors/actresses. These cas
dedicated himself to a spe
senting child actors/actres

"Robert Pafundi went abov
come was outstanding. His
his willingness to find a wa
it could not be won, are wha
I highly recommend him an

"For more than a dozen yea
ment industry cases with Ro
ing and his ethics are impecc
*Safe Stardom*, Mr. Pafundi is,
the law regarding children in
sive, even to many attorneys.
tertainment Laws comes fron
one of Hollywood's most histc
specialized in the representatic
Manager Association-endorsed
pled with his over 25 years of
in understanding the industry f
negotiating TV and Motion Pict

"Mr. Pafundi is also an outstanc
ners in litigation. What I find far
disputes by negotiation or medi
suming expense, and the often j
troversies that make their way to

several very high
the benefits of his
In addition, he is

"After all the worl
Entertainment L
book, *Safe Stard*
when it came to
*Safe Stardom* wil
ily from making

"Robert has wor
say he really has
and presenting i
vided me with
options, and his
with various lav
knowledgeable
a rare quality ar
Last, but certair

"Robert Pafunc
extremely kno
regard to Tale
pleasure of wo
ment matters
—Elizab

"I've known R
ate. His skills
a man of the
his results an
opponents as
understands

# SAFE STARDOM

# SAFE STARDOM

How to *Protect* Your Children on
Their Road to Fame

Hollywood Entertainment Lawyer
Robert Pafundi

Foreword by Caitlin Sanchez
Voice of *Dora The Explorer*™

DUNHAM
*books*

*Safe Stardom*
© 2014 Robert Pafundi

### *Safe Stardom* Cover Photography

Photograph of Jordy Roth by Michael Dambrosia Photo,
2519 S Westgate Avenue, Los Angeles, CA 90064 Telephone: 310-444-7391
Website: http://www.michaeldambrosia.com

Photograph of Catherine Chan by Karl Preston Photography,
Santa Monica, CA 90405 Telephone: 310.396.9733
Website: http://www.KarlPreston.com

Photograph of Sienna Lavigne by her mother, Melissa Lavigne.

Photograph of Craig Traylor by Shawn Barber Photography,
West Hollywood, CA 90069 Telephone: 818-261-5025
Website: www.HeadshotsDoneRight.com

Photograph of Daniela Jette by Paul Smith Photography,
2020 North Main Street, Suite 241, Los Angeles, CA 90031
Telephone: 323-463-8864 Website: http://www.paulsmithphotography.com

Hardcover: 978-1-939447-34-0
Ebook: 978-1-939447-35-7

*Printed in the United States of America*

# Dedication

*To my mother, Vannina "Vee" Pafundi, who has always believed in me and taught me the definition of unconditional love.*

*To my father, Victor "Big Vic" Pafundi, who is always there when I need him.*

*To my children, Alexandra "Alex" and Nicholas "Nick" who, without conscious awareness, are my inspiration.*

*To all the children who will defy the odds and dare to live your dream, I applaud you; I admire you; and I will be there to protect you.*

# Disclaimer

As an attorney licensed to practice law, Robert Pafundi has filled the pages that follow with important and valuable information related to the protection and representation of children in entertainment. However, what you're holding in your hands is still a book and not an attorney, so with it comes some built-in limitations.

Robert Pafundi is licensed to practice law in the State of California, USA, and the laws that he refers to in this book, unless specifically stated, are only applicable in California. Every reader should keep in mind that entertainment-related business practices and laws differ greatly from country to country and even from state to state. Also, laws in today's world change frequently and can be subject to numerous exceptions, so readers should not act or rely on any information in this book without first seeking the advice of an attorney. Neither Robert Pafundi, as author, and/or his publisher guarantee that anyone following the techniques, suggestions, tips, ideas, or strategies in this book will successfully resolve any legal issue or entertainment industry matter.

The purpose of this book is to educate and entertain. The information in these pages does not constitute legal advice, nor should it be considered as a substitute for the personalized advice of a lawyer. This book is not intended to create an attorney-client relationship, which can only be created by entering a written retainer agreement signed by all parties.

This book uses actual and hypothetical examples that feature parents, children, Talent Managers, Talent Agents, producers, and other entertainment companies to illustrate certain legal issues. Other than in matters of public record, names have been changed. The use of these names and marks does not imply any approval, sponsorship, or affiliation with the owners or these trademarks. A similar case does not mean identical cases. Often, a small nuance in the facts can change the outcome.

The author nor his publisher shall have neither liability nor responsibility to anyone with respect to any loss or damage caused, or alleged to be caused, directly or indirectly by the information contained in this book. Additionally, they shall not be liable for the readers' misuse of this material. All views expressed in this book are those of the author and do not necessarily reflect those of the publisher or anyone he consulted while writing this book.

It is the author's sincere and honest intent that you learn from these pages and find great value in the information that follows.

# CONTENTS

# On the Cover of *Safe Stardom*

*Safe Stardom* was written for parents and children from all walks of life and all ages and ethnicities. It is for those who have just started to dream of a career in acting to those with years of training and experience, and for families and children everywhere in between.

The kids on the cover of *Safe Stardom* were carefully hand-selected to reflect the fact that this book was written to help families and children of all ages and cultures—all of you. Without question, the children of many of my readers could grace the cover of this book, and I hope to meet you and your children in my travels, but for today let me tell you about the five Stars on the cover of *Safe Stardom*. From left to right, they are:

- **Jordy Roth,** an aspiring actor who has performed on live stage and has also auditioned for National commercials.

- The beautiful and talented **Catherine Chan** is an up-and-coming Star, who played the lead young female, opposite Jason Statham, in the IMG-produced Major Motion Picture, *Safe*, an action crime thriller directed by Boaz Yakin (*Now You See Me*) and produced by Dana Brunetti (*The Social Network*). She has also appeared in a Guest Star Role on the hit TV Series, *Weeds*. Catherine is now a local hire in New York.

- **Sienna Lavigne,** who just turned five, is just a bit older than this adorable picture. She is represented by DDO Artists Agency and has appeared in *Fit Pregnancy* magazine as a print model. Sienna regularly auditions and trains in her school drama class. Outside of her love for acting, she loves riding horses, swimming, and playing with her friends, and volunteers at the local pet shelters. We expect to see her very soon on both live stage and in Motion Pictures as she develops her career.

- Next, did you recognize the now tall, handsome, and much older **Craig Lamar Traylor,** whose real-life journey was my inspiration for writing *Safe Stardom*? As you will learn, or be reminded when you read this book, Craig started his acting career at age five and quickly booked many National TV Commercials, a role in the mega-hit comedy by TriStar Pictures, *Matilda*, and ultimately played the quirky and often hilarious Stevie Kenarban in 56 episodes of the FOX hit TV show, *Malcolm in the Middle.*

- **Daniela Jette** is a stunning SAG-AFTRA actress who booked her first commercials as a seven-year-old! She is fluent in English and Spanish, super-athletic, and a highly skilled singer and guitarist. Most recently, she signed with the Daniel Hoff Agency, Los Angeles. Daniela has worked on live stage and trained with some of the best in the industry, including Cynthia Bain in Los Angeles, and at the New York Film Academy. To keep things even more fun and interesting, Daniela has become more involved in her singing/songwriting and she even started performing acoustic shows at local coffee shops, as well as attending music school.

# How to Use This Book

*Everything should be made as simple as possible,*
*but not simpler.*

–Albert Einstein

*Safe Stardom* can be read on many levels. It is the story of one mother and son, how they made it in Hollywood, and how they changed the entertainment industry in the process. It is also a resource for parents and children who are involved, or aspire to be, in the entertainment industry. This book distills a tremendous amount of information that is helpful to parents and their children—information that I have learned over the course of more than a dozen years as a Talent Agent, Talent Manager, and entertainment lawyer.

*Safe Stardom* is divided into seven parts, each of which addresses one aspect of the world in which children and entertainment operate. Parts I and II provide general, practical, and legal background about the roles and responsibilities of the Hollywood insiders—Talent Agents, Talent Managers, and entertainment lawyers—who shape the careers of children and young adults in Hollywood. These parts of the book will be useful to parents who are new to entertainment as well as those who have experience dealing with talents agents and Talent Managers.

Parts III through VII describe various aspects of working with these professionals, and are organized chronologically beginning with how to hire them, what to look for in their contracts, how to work with them productively, and what do to if the relationship breaks down and comes to an end—either by mutual agreement or in a lawsuit or related dispute.

## There are at Least Four Different
## Ways to Read This Book.

If you or your child are in a particular phase of dealing with a Talent Agent or Talent Manager, you will get the most out of reading the corresponding portion of the book. Thus, for example, if you are already a member of the SAG-AFTRA guild and have a question about union pay scales on movies and TV shows, read Part IV—Compensation. Likewise, if you are unhappy with a talent manger or agent and are

### A NOTE ABOUT CAPITALIZATION

*Throughout the book you will notice that certain words are capitalized in ways that violate the rules that we were taught by our fourth-grade teachers. For example, Series Regular, Artist, and Agreement. These terms and phrases are often capitalized in entertainment contracts; one of the purposes of this book is to shed light on how the entertainment industry views the business world and writes about it. That is why certain words are capitalized as they are.*

contemplating making a change, please read Part VI, which describes how business relationships end in the entertainment industry.

If you are primarily interested in following the story of Craig and MeShiel, the mother and son alluded to above, read the first chapter of each of the first six parts of the book, as well as Part VII.

*Safe Stardom* is also a guide to entertainment contracts, especially contracts involving Talent Agents and Talent Managers. The book contains more than two dozen provisions that commonly appear in such contracts, along with commentary about the purpose, benefits, and drawbacks of different contractual provisions.

*Safe Stardom* is much more than a book about Entertainment Law. It addresses a wide range of issues that relate to protecting our children in Hollywood, including protecting them from overly aggressive paparazzi and sexual predators. You will find this information in Part V.

We all have a stake in protecting the children who work or aspire to work in the entertainment industry. I hope that, whatever your involvement or experience with the entertainment industry, you will find this book useful.

If you have any questions or comments about any aspect of *Safe Stardom*, I encourage you to contact me at the email address listed below.

Robert Pafundi
Los Angeles, California
Robert@SafeStardom.com

# FOREWORD

When Robert Pafundi told me that he was going to write a book that focused on educating parents and protecting child performers in the entertainment industry, it immediately struck a chord with me. You see, I am one of those child performers. I began working in the industry at the tender age of eight, auditioning for commercials as well as scripted television roles. I've even appeared on NBC's *Law & Order: SVU*. But my real big break came in animated television at the ripe old age of eleven. I was the voice actress for the title character on Nickelodeon's *Dora the Explorer*. Since then, millions of people around the world have heard my voice daily, and as I approach eighteen, they continue to hear my voice on television, the Internet, video games, and toys.

The entertainment industry offers so much potential for the talented, but it is also filled with potential pitfalls for the ill-informed. Hollywood is teeming with complexities and challenges for any aspiring child performer, from dealing with guilds, Talent Agents, and Talent Managers to the production companies themselves, and you, as a parent, owe it to yourself and your child to learn the dynamic interrelationships that are so clearly explained in this book.

My parents and I did not have a blueprint or an in-depth understanding of the entertainment industry when I began. A book just like this would have been invaluable, as I was navigating my way through the labyrinth that is Hollywood.

Fortunately, with this book in hand, you can take advice and guidance from Robert Pafundi, an experienced former Talent Agent, Talent Manager, and successful entertainment attorney and litigator who is dedicated to fighting for the rights of children in the entertainment industry. What makes this book unique and vital to all parents of child performers entering into the industry is that it finally puts the spotlight on the rights and laws that exist to protect child performers; these rights and laws, while not exactly "hidden," have never surfaced at any "Hollywood 101" class that I've attended. This book goes beyond the acting class seminars, the talent showcase meet-and-greets, and the smiling faces you encounter; it teaches you all you need to know about the nuances and intricacies of the business and how to protect your child in the process.

What Robert has depicted in *Safe Stardom* is of the utmost importance to families embarking on a performing career. Why? Because when you enter the entertainment industry, you and your child are inherently at a disadvantage. You can't take full advantage of the wonderful opportunities that Hollywood offers until you know the roles of the people whom you are dealing with, and exactly how to interact and work with them. Your greatest asset in the entertainment industry is not how talented your child is, but rather how well informed you are as a parent. This book provides details and knowledge about all entertainment industry players who will impact your child's career path in a readily understandable manner that both newcomers and experienced talent will appreciate.

In between taking your child to auditions and hoping for callbacks, you should be reading this book and assimilating its information. Take it from me, an experienced child performer: never underestimate the business side of show business. Everybody loves a star; so dare to dream as I have done, but recognize the reality of the entertainment world and educate yourself so that you can safely navigate the mazes of Hollywood. You can do that by reading *Safe Stardom*.

**—Caitlin Sanchez**
**Former Voice Actress of Nickelodeon's *Dora the Explorer*™**

Not only *could* it happen to an entertainment child and his mother—it did.

Imagine this scenario: Your ten-year-old son or daughter finally gets a big break and books a Series Regular role on a TV show for a major television network, or a lead role in a Motion Picture. Then, a few years later, while still acting in that role, your child is sued for breach of contract, and before you know it, a court enters a judgment for over half a million dollars against you and your child. Imagine the confusion, fear and panic. How could this happen?

Unfortunately, this is exactly what happened to a well-known child actor who one day was happily on the set working as a Series Regular on a hit TV show for the FOX Television Network; the next he found himself and his family in a major legal dispute with his Talent Manager. The lawsuit was initiated by the manager—someone the child's family considered a friend. This well-known Los Angeles talent management company accused the child and his mother of "illegally" violating the terms of a contract signed several years prior. Instead of going to court, the contract provided that the matter be decided by a privately appointed arbitrator. This is a common practice, as most arbitrations are private matters and do not become part of the public record. However, at the hearings, the Talent Manager made accusations that would not have had a chance of standing up in court, but a careless arbitrator believed those charges; a trial judge blindly confirmed them, and with that, the court entered a judgment against both the mother and child actor for well over $500,000.

After this all transpired, I was asked to represent that little boy and his mother. We fought back against the injustice. We fought back against the stupidity. It took several years, but we made people listen. We fought back and said, "This is not right." We forced people in a position of authority to take action on our charge, "Who's Protecting the Children?" Fortunately, the Justices of the Court of Appeal answered *unanimously* that they would indeed protect our children.

*Safe Stardom*, a book I wrote out of fervor and necessity, outlines this specific case. But more importantly, it not only summarizes the legal repercussions and its aftermath; it goes well beyond that, so you, your family, and all of those involved in the world of child actors, from the talent themselves, to parents, Talent Managers, Talent Agents, and the lawyers for all of them, have a clear understanding of what is involved in representing Hollywood's children.

Of far greater significance than winning the case (well, maybe not for the mother and her child), I discovered several little-known things in the process that should greatly benefit any parent and child in the entertainment business. I discovered what it takes to protect your family and your children. I discovered that with persistence, mistaken legal opinions are correctable, and more importantly, horror stories like this can be prevented. Join me as I tell you what happened and how you can make sure something like this never happens to you and your child.

This book was written for you, the parent of a child actor or child hopeful, to prepare and educate you—in plain and simple English—as to how to navigate those difficult waters of making "legal" decisions for your child and his/her career. I wrote this book to fill a void and answer questions created by our ever-changing world where virtually every decision, and certainly every business decision, has some legal ramification attached to it. I wrote this book because, as a parent, former Screen Actor's Guild-franchised Talent Agent, Talent Manager, and long-time entertainment attorney, I know firsthand how hard it is to do it all, and do it all alone. However, with some knowledge, guidance, and advice, you can be better prepared and better equipped and that is why *Safe Stardom* was written.

Here, in this book, you'll come to better understand the law and the many practical sides of the industry that you may not have ever even thought about before, and you will walk away feeling not only more comfortable as you move forward with your child's career, but also save your family a lot of potential heartache as you and your child take on the challenges and joys of Hollywood.

# PART I

*How Talent Agents, Talent Managers, and Entertainment Lawyers Shape the Careers of Hollywood Kids*

# CHAPTER 1

## THE MOTHER AND SON WHO CHANGED HOLLYWOOD

*A mother's love for her child is like nothing else in the world. It knows no law, no pity. It dares all things and crushes down remorselessly all that stands in its path.*

—Agatha Christie

When Craig Traylor was three years old, he watched the classic Disney movie, *The Little Mermaid*. His mother, MeShiel, looked on as Craig pretended to be one of the main characters, assigned roles to his friends, told them what to say, and helped them with their lines. "How precious," MeShiel thought. And like many other parents, she allowed herself a fleeting thought; "Maybe my child will be in Hollywood someday." And then she forgot about it and returned to the day-to-day details of her life.

MeShiel worked as a professional youth counselor, placing disadvantaged children in more suitable home environments. She and her husband lived in Riverside, California, a fast-growing city of 300,000 in the heart of the Inland Empire, about a two-hour drive from Hollywood. Craig was their first child.

Several months later, MeShiel was shopping with Craig in a local mall. He needed new glasses. As they were walking through the mall on the way back to their car, a woman commented about Craig's glasses. That triggered a great conversation.

Unbeknownst to MeShiel or Craig, the woman worked for a talent search company. She asked Craig if he would like do some modeling; he would dress in nice clothes—sometimes even a tuxedo—and go on stage in front of lots of people.

A week later, Craig entered his first modeling competition. It was a small, local event. He won. This quickly led to a national competition held 45 minutes away in Palm Springs. Craig won again.

Craig's dream of "being on TV" was soon to become a reality. After Palm Springs, countless modeling and Talent Agents approached MeShiel. Craig signed up with a well-known, full-service agency representing children and adults in on-camera commercials, TV, and Film.

Craig started going to auditions and within a few months appeared in a seasonal television commercial starring Annette Funicello. One of his older co-stars was Mila Kunis, who was only eight years old at the time. This, in turn, led to a series of commercials, including a run of commercials for McDonald's.

Within a year, with MeShiel's guidance and his charismatic personality, Craig signed with the highly regarded Osbrink Agency, which represents Dakota Fanning, Kaitlyn Dever, and other stars. There, he achieved early Film and TV success. Craig made his first appearance on a TV show at age 5 in a scene with George Clooney on the highly acclaimed prime-time hit TV show *ER*. By age 7, Craig appeared in the feature film, *Matilda*, starring Danny DeVito, who handpicked Craig for his role in the movie. And this was just the beginning; Craig later became a Series Regular on a hit TV series.

MeShiel and Craig Traylor represent the aspirations of millions of families who dream about Hollywood and how it can transform their lives. Craig's story is also one of extraordinary accomplishment. Craig Traylor didn't become a huge celebrity. His isn't a household name. Chances are good that you've never heard of him. But Craig was more successful than 99 percent of boys and girls under the age of 18 who go to auditions or otherwise try to make it the entertainment business. By any reasonable measure, Craig made it big in Hollywood.

But that is not the most remarkable part of Craig and MeShiel's story. That is not what makes their story worth telling—although it's a great story of good people overcoming obstacles and beating the odds. It's not why other parents and their children can learn so much from Craig and MeShiel.

MeShiel and Craig managed to do something even the most famous stars rarely succeed in doing. The entertainment business is notorious for being tough on families, and potentially harmful to kids. It's not hard to think of child stars who couldn't handle fame and fortune, and who flamed out as young adults. The tabloids and glossy weekly magazines are full of stories of their financial struggles and misfortunes with drugs, alcohol, and divorce. These are stories of how Hollywood changes people—generally for the worse.

But, as you shall see, Hollywood didn't change them; instead, MeShiel and Craig Traylor changed Hollywood...for the better.

# CHAPTER 2

## THE LEGAL AND PRACTICAL DIFFERENC ESBETWEEN TALENT AGENTS AND TALENT MANAGERS

*The division largely exists only in theory. The reality is not nearly so neat. The line dividing the functions of agents... and managers... is often blurred and sometimes crossed.*

—Hon. Kathryn M. Werdegar, Justice,
California Supreme Court
*Marathon Entertainment v. Rosa Blasi*

If your child seriously considers a career in the entertainment business—whether in television, feature Films, commercials, or live stage—you, as the parent or guardian, need to appreciate fully the legal and practical day-to-day differences between a Talent Agent and a Talent Manager. Even agents and managers sometimes have difficulty agreeing, among themselves, on who does what, and whether an actor even needs both representatives. But it's important to keep the distinction between managers and agents clear. This clarity can help you and your child save thousands of dollars, earn more roles and money, avoid conflicts or even lawsuits, and otherwise protect your child.

Fortunately, the California Supreme Court in 2008 provided a very useful shorthand definition of the difference between Talent Agents and Talent Managers:

- Agents procure roles; they put artists on the screen, on the stage, behind the camera; and, *according to the law, only they may do so.*

- Managers coordinate everything else; they counsel and advise, take care of business arrangements, and chart the course of an artist's career.

Although the reality of how Hollywood works isn't so clean cut, one of the basic distinctions, legally, between Talent Agents and Talent Managers is that in California only Talent Agents are legally authorized to find work for their clients. In fact, Talent Managers can get into trouble and harm your child's career if they cross the line and find work for him or her. The technical term for finding work is "procurement," and Chapter 4 discusses what happens if Talent Managers improperly procure work.

Several important practical differences result from the fact that only agents are legally authorized to procure work. Talent Agents are sometimes described as the foot soldiers who slog through the trenches of Hollywood. Beyond this romantic view, an agent's job is three-tiered. First, agents are responsible for keeping tabs on trends and developments in the business. Second, they send clients on auditions and generally represent talent in opportunities that will, hopefully, lead to work on television, print ads, commercials, Major Motion Pictures or the live stage. Third, if someone (a producer, for example) wants to book a deal, a TV show, a movie, a commercial, or live stage theater project, the agent (or lawyer) will negotiate the "deal points." This is the name that is commonly given to the most important elements of the contract, and will be discussed in detail in Chapter 21.

## AGENTS IN A NUTSHELL

- Under California law, Talent Agents must be licensed and bonded by the State. The license application process is complex and elaborate. It requires the submission of substantial personal information, references, FBI fingerprinting and clearing a background check, the payment of annual fees and the securing of a $50,000 renewal bond.

- All Talent Agents in California are regulated by the *Talent Agencies Act of California*—the TAA.

- Talent Agents are also regulated by the various unions (oftentimes called Guilds) that represent most of the talent in Hollywood: Screen Actors Guild (SAG), American Federation of Television and Radio Artists (AFTRA, now SAG-AFTRA), Directors Guild of America (DGA), Writers Guild of America (WGA), and American Federation of Musicians (AFM).

- Many Talent Agents operate under the Screen Actors Guild (SAG) franchise agreement, utilizing SAG contracts. Alternatively, others are members of the breakaway Association of Talent Agents (ATA). The differences between the two are discussed in Chapter 3.

- Talent Agents earn a commission if their client is booked as a direct result of their submission, pitch, or meeting with a casting director or producer. Because of the influence of the various guilds, agents' commissions are often capped—up to 10% on work an actor books on union TV, Film and commercials, and up to 20% on print work. Although fees for non-union projects are unregulated, it is rare for agents' commissions to exceed 20%.

- Talent Agents typically ask an actor to sign a one-year contract, which often includes a performance-based "bailout" or "exit" clause, allowing the actor to terminate the contract if the agent does not secure work for the actor after, for example, 120 days.

- Talent Agents have input on an actor's headshots, but rarely have the time to work through hundreds of shots from a photography session.

- Good agents submit electronic or hard-copy photographs, resumes and biographies, *and* pitch verbally to get the actors they represent "in the door" with casting directors.

- Talent Agents, by definition, negotiate deals when an actor books the part, which includes trying to enhance and improve the basic elements of the agreement, such as the length of the agreement and level of compensation.

## How Talent Managers Are Different

Managers, by contrast, are completely unregulated. They can choose to become members of private organizations such as the *Talent Managers Association* (TMA) and the *National Conference of Personal Managers* (NCOPM) and abide by those organizations' specific codes of ethics or rules of conduct. However, even some of Hollywood's top Talent Managers choose not to join these organizations, so membership is not a guarantee of either credibility or ability.

Talent Managers offer a broader array of services than do agents. They focus on advising each client on long-term career goals, with the aim of making them as marketable as possible. They often manage their clients' personal *and* professional lives. This has been known to include, in certain rare circumstances, lending money to and acting as a spokesperson on behalf of their clients. Managers may also act as producers, including producing some or all of their client's work.

## TALENT MANAGERS IN A NUTSHELL

- Talent Managers invest a great deal of time and energy into an actor's *potential*, often long before the actor has a track record of booking consistently.

- Managers are largely unregulated, but can elect to be members of the TMA or NCOPM, both of which have specific codes of conduct for members.

- Many managers earn as much as fifteen percent (15%) commission on all work booked.

Because their role in an actor's career is more personal than an agent's role, Talent Managers typically request a longer contract term, up to three years, and occasionally even longer. Furthermore, they often expect to work for actors for quite some time before seeing any return at all on their investment.

A good Talent Manager can make a significant difference in the development, growth, and maintenance of an actor's career. Most legitimate, professional Talent Managers are people who are nurturing by nature. It is not only the new or young actors who benefit from this. Many seasoned actors have enjoyed the benefits of this career assistance throughout various stages of their working lives. The key words, however, are "legitimate" and "professional." Since Talent Managers, unlike Talent Agents, are not regulated, there is more room for the unscrupulous.

## THE DIFFERENCE BETWEEN TALENT AGENTS
## AND TALENT MANAGERS IN CALIFORNIA

| Subject Matter of Differences | Talent Agents | Talent Managers |
|---|---|---|
| Primary Purpose of Representation | Submit Your Child to Casting Directors and Producers. Pitch, negotiate, book and close deals. | Offer valuable career guidance advice. Work closely with or even find the perfect agent, and focus on long-term career goals. |
| License Required by the State (Based on a submitted application) | Yes | No |
| Insurance Bond of $50,000 required by the State (Designed to protect actors) | Yes | No |
| May legally procure work for Actors (i.e., submit to Casting Directors and Producers. Pitch your child, negotiate, book and close deals). | Yes | No (Although Know to Effectively Submit and Pitch Actors) |
| Regulated by specific statutes (The Talent Agencies Act [TAA], California Labor Code §§ 1700, et seq.) | Yes | No (Although can be subjected to civil prosecution for violation of the TAA) |
| Operate or Contract with Talent Using Union/Guild Franchise or Similar Agreements (SAG, AFTRA, ATA) | Yes | No |
| Membership in organization or groups promoting ethical code of conduct (i.e., Talent Managers Association and/or National Conference of Personal Managers) | Membership not open to Talent Agents | Some Join (Membership not required, nor true indication of competence) |
| Commissions charged must be Pre-Approved by State License Division | Yes | No |
| Commission Percentages charged on SAG-AFTRA or union projects (Percentage must be pre-approved by State License Division) | Up to 10% for TV, Film and Commercial | Unregulated. Typically 15% but Ranges from 10% to 20% |
| Commission percentage charged on non-union, non-jurisdictional and print projects (Percentage must be pre-approved by State License Division) | Up to 20% | Unregulated. Typically 15% but ranges from 10% to 20% |
| Length of Contract | Typically one year (includes 120-day exit clause) | Typically three years (often with various types of renewal provisions) |
| Can petition the court for approval of contract entered with minor | Yes | No |

*There's no right or wrong, success or failure. I don't look at things as black or white. My life won't be a series of either/ors—musician or actor, rock or country, straitlaced or rebellious, this or that, yes or no. The real choices in life aren't that simple.*

—Miley Cyrus

The subject of the different types of Talent Agents actually presents two very distinct issues.

First is the issue that seems to raise the most confusion among almost all actors and actresses—that of understanding the distinction between a Talent Agent who is "franchised" by the Screen Actors Guild (a SAG Franchised Agency) and one affiliated with the Association of Talent Agents (an ATA Talent Agency). This chapter will discuss the important differences between the two.

Second is the unrelated issue dealing with the categories of talent agency representation that exist. This type of representation is much more related to your child's goals and dreams in the entertainment world. For example, if your child wants to try a career "in the movies," he would seek a "theatrical agent," whereas if she wants to be a high fashion model, she would seek a modeling agency, and a particular one at that. A wide selection of agency categories are both identified and explained in the second half of this chapter.

## IS YOUR CHILD'S AGENT A SAG-AFTRA FRANCHISED TALENT AGENCY OR AN ATA TALENT AGENCY? WHAT'S THE DIFFERENCE AND DOES IT REALLY MATTER?

Let's clear up the confusion surrounding this important issue, and help you decide if one is better or more legitimate than the other.

There are two types of agencies. There are those franchised with SAG-AFTRA and those affiliated with the ATA. Making a choice would therefore seemingly be very simple. However, the truth is, due to the inherent complexities in talent agency relations today a little understanding of this will go a long way to your feeling better about which type of agency you choose for your child.

For our discussion here, what a parent needs to know is that an agency qualifies as a SAG-AFTRA-Franchised Agency by having an application approved by the SAG-AFTRA Agency Department. The application requires, among several important things, evidence that the agent or agency is licensed by the State where it does business. Alternatively, Talent Agents and agencies can become a Member of the ATA by completing an ATA Application for Membership, which likewise requires, among other things, evidence that the agent or agency is licensed by the State where it does business. While, for the most part, this means a presence in California or New York, the ATA, like SAG, certainly has a presence in other states. The ATA Board of Directors must approve all applications for membership, and the agents or agencies that join must pay dues to maintain active membership.

So what's the fuss about whether your agent or agency is SAG-franchised or an ATA Member?

### SAG-Franchised Talent Agents

To summarize, the Screen Actors Guild (SAG), established in 1933, was, until very recently, the nation's largest labor union representing working actors. It recently merged with the nation's second largest labor union for actors, The American Federation of Television and Radio Artists (AFTRA), creating SAG-AFTRA, which is now the largest labor union in the world of entertainment. A full discussion of Hollywood Labor Unions and the impact of the merger can be found in Chapter 22.

In the past, before 2002, all SAG-franchised Talent Agents were legally obligated to abide by the requirements of what is known as SAG's "Rule 16(g)"— a term you will likely hear being tossed about if you are in the business long enough. Rule 16(g) is technically known as the "SAG Agency Franchise Agreement," but almost everyone refers to it by the rule number, its well-established nickname. The rule governs the relationship between the Screen Actors Guild and those Talent Agents "franchised" by SAG. If your agent is franchised by SAG, then your agent (as well as the SAG actors and actresses they represent) continue to be protected by and bound to the terms and conditions of Rule 16(g). In short, this would include the interpretation and enforcement of all of SAG's regulations and contracts, including, of course, talent agency contracts with actors and actresses.

In 2002, the Agreement expired. Negotiations to adopt a newer, current version failed. When the Agreement expired, the SAG Board voted to temporarily suspend the enforcement of Section 16(a) of SAG's Rules and Regulations that required all SAG actors and actresses to "sign" with SAG-franchised agents only. This temporary suspension, however, *only* applies to ATA agents who were formally franchised, meaning that SAG actors and actresses could choose, but only between the two.

Thus a divide was created at that time, which still exists today, between those agents who decided to remain loyal to SAG (meaning to voluntarily honor Rule 16[g] and remain franchised despite the lack of a written agreement) and those who decided to move away and join the ATA agents who are no longer SAG-franchised. So, yes, it was (and still is) considered a big deal to many, because SAG cannot enforce its agency rules against ATA agencies, limiting what it (SAG) can do to help protect your children (or adults) who sign with ATA agencies.

Hundreds of SAG-franchised agents across the country have maintained their on-going relationship with SAG in this fashion, and continue to serve SAG's members under the requirements of Rule 16(g). And, a big part of this is that *all* SAG-AFTRA-franchised Talent Agents are obligated to use pre-approved SAG-AFTRA contracts that comply with Rule 16(g) whenever they "sign" actors they wish to represent for TV, Film, or commercials. SAG claims that its franchised agents are unmatched when it comes to protecting SAG actors, because of the Rule 16(g) requirements to which the agents must adhere and because SAG can help enforce the Rule should a dispute arise.

### ATA Talent Agents

The ATA (which generally also includes Talent Agents affiliated with the National Association of Talent Representatives ["NATR"] is a nonprofit trade association that was founded in 1937. It boasts of representing "the finest talent agencies in the industry" and being "the voice of unified talent and literary agencies." The ATA states that its Member Agencies represent the vast majority of working artists, including actors, directors, writers, and other artists in Film, stage, television, radio, commercials, literary work, and other entertainment enterprises. If you would like to learn more about the ATA or for a current (and very impressive) list of ATA Talent Agents, visit the online website, noted at the end of this chapter.

## A SAG-Franchised Agency and ATA Agency Contracts With Your Child: A Comparison

SAG takes the position that a fundamental difference between it and the ATA is that ATA agents have no legal obligation to abide by the requirements of Rule 16(g), the SAG Agency Franchise Agreement. SAG adds that, as a result, it cannot protect actors against those ATA agents who deviate from its provisions or offer contracts that are contrary to its rules, leaving actors and actresses to fend for themselves if a dispute arises. The ATA assures that all of its agencies continue to work with actors under ATA state-approved agency contracts, and that ATA agents "have worked in partnership with artists and their guilds to ensure their protection and promote their creative endeavors."

SAG, however, is troubled that actors and actresses who sign with ATA talent agencies are typically asked to sign "General Services Agreements" (GSAs a.k.a. "Talent Agency Agreements") and SAG believes that some GSAs "do not conform to the terms and conditions of SAG Rule 16(g), whittle away your bargaining power, and should be carefully scrutinized." Here are a few of the particulars that concern SAG about ATA General Service Agreements that may be presented to your child for signature:

- A GSA could make *all* of an actor's income commissionable, whereas SAG-Franchised Agents operating under Rule 16(g) have strict guidelines regarding income from which they are forbidden from taking a commission;

- A GSA could, if the ATA agency chose, restrict an actor's ability to engage separate representation for different areas of work (e.g., restrict your choice to have a separate agent for Commercials and TV/Film), whereas SAG-Franchised Agents are obligated to offer flexibility to actors when it comes to engaging separate representation;

- A GSA could limit both series performers' and day players' ability to terminate an agency contract based on lack of employment or even an agent's material breach of said contract;

- A GSA could restrict an Actor's ability to engage the services of a personal manager or an attorney.

These concerns by SAG don't automatically mean SAG-Franchised Agents are necessarily better than the ATA Agents—not at all. Even

SAG states that if an actor elects an ATA agency and is presented with a GSA, the actor should simply: (1) "Attempt to negotiate terms and conditions that are similar to, or better than, those in the standard SAG Agency Agreement" and (2) "Seek independent legal advice prior to signing any contract that is NOT a SAG Contract."

In the end, while my talent agency (MGA—Mary Grady Talent Agency, as it was known) elected to remain a loyal SAG franchise, my experience has shown me that actors and actresses who heed the above warnings when entering talent agency contracts have had very satisfying relationships and great results with both SAG-Franchised and ATA Agencies. The key is to understand with whom you are working, more so than some "black and white" rule of preference because, as explained throughout this book, there are many other factors that go into this decision.

## IS YOUR CHILD REPRESENTED BY AN AGENT WHO FITS WITH HIS OR HER ASPIRATIONS AND GOALS?

Next, as you navigate the options of the many categories of Talent Agents available to your child, some of these descriptions of the most common types of representation will be very valuable in deciding which type of agent is best suited to help your child reach his or her goals and dreams.

### *Theatrical Agent*

A theatrical agent usually concentrates on helping actors and actresses book roles in Film and television, and sometimes theatre. This would include "on camera" roles for both independent movies and Major Motion Pictures produced by the studios (i.e., Warner Bros., DreamWorks, Paramount, etc.), as well as "on camera" sitcoms and dramatic episodic television, Movies of the Week (MOWs), and Soap Operas. Some theatrical agents also seek roles for live stage and live theatre performances in Equity plays, whether booking such roles in a well-regarded Los Angeles venue, like The Ahmanson Theatre, or for a Broadway Play in New York City. Some people describe agents who focus exclusively on musical theatre, live stage plays, and choir productions as "Legit Agents," meaning "Legitimate Stage," which does not necessarily refer to the agent's moral or ethical qualities. This term is not used very frequently anymore, at least not in California.

### Commercial Agent

A commercial agent generally focuses on representing talent and arranging auditions for "on camera" local, regional, national, seasonal (holiday), and international television commercials. Commercial agents will also seek auditions for Public Service Announcements (PSAs) and corporate and educational pieces generally created and produced by larger companies and corporations to educate its employees or corporate affiliates. Included in this category are, of course, auditions for ongoing commercial spots, well known as Commercial Campaigns, or just Campaigns.

### Print Agent

A print agent represents up-and-coming and already successful talent for commercials and advertisements shown in, for example, local, national and international magazines, newspapers, Internet promotions and ads, catalogues, billboards, direct mail advertising, packaging on retail products often sold throughout the world, and even textbooks. Print agents generally differ from modeling agents, discussed below, in that print agents typically help fill the enormous need for those who look like "real people," or those who convey a sense of "trust and honesty" or, alternatively, those who portray a "quirky" or a particular "character" look.

### Modeling Agent

A modeling agent can overlap to some degree with a Print Agent; however, true to form, "Modeling" agents generally focus on "high fashion" or "elite fashion" models for specialized work in print and television commercials for companies like Victoria's Secret, Gucci, Calvin Klein, Prada, and Giorgio Armani, to name a few. Modeling agents also book their models for both live and TV "Runway" modeling events. Some of the world's top modeling agencies include Ford Models, with offices in 10 major cities throughout the world, Elite Model Management, with offices in 6 major markets, IMG Models, similarly situated, and NEXT Model Management, with offices in New York and Paris, although many other excellent modeling agencies certainly exist.

### Voice-Over Agent

A voice-over agent represents talent for roles in Film, television, commercials, and radio advertisements. While many actors want to be seen *and* heard, others have made lucrative careers in voice-over work, for things like the voice of an unseen narrator speaking in the background, the voice of a visible character (as in a Motion Picture) expressing unspoken thoughts, the voice of an animated character (like the work of Jack Black or Angelina Jolie voicing the characters in DreamWorks's productions of *Kung Fu Panda,* or that of Caitlin Sanchez who performed for over three years as the title character, Dora, on Nickelodeon's *Dora the Explorer*), or playing the roles of robotic characters like R2-D2 and C-3PO in the six Lucasfilms productions of *Star Wars*.

## Literary Agent

A literary agent (often synonymous with a publishing agent) is an agent who represents writers and their written works in presentations and pitches to publishers, theatrical producers and Film producers. They often assist in the sale and deal negotiation of their written works. Literary agents most often represent novelists, screenwriters and non-fiction writers. Quite a few well-known, powerful, and lucrative publishing houses do not accept submissions from those who are not represented by a literary agent.

## Music Agents and Managers

Although music is not the focus of this book, in the music world, music booking agents are different from Talent Agents who represent actors and actresses for TV, Film, and commercials. Music booking agents are those who actually "book" shows for the musical artists they represent. They make all of the arrangements with the promoters of the shows. The booking agent presents the promoter or producer of a concert, for example, with a written agreement, which details the musical artist's requirements, including things like lighting, sound, meals, hotel accommodations, and transportation. For concert buyers, they work to find the right artist who will fit the need and available budget. Many of the major music booking agencies refuse to represent artists who are not already signed to a major record label and have national or international distribution of their music. Because of this, artists on smaller independent record labels often seek representation with an independent booking agency. Conversely, a music manager (or band manager) handles many career issues for bands and singers and, on occasion, even DJs.

A music manager is also very different from a Talent Manager who represents actors and actresses for TV, Film and commercials, as he or she is hired by a musician or band to help with determining decisions related to career moves, bookings, promotions, business deals, recording contracts, etc. The role of a music manager is extensive and may include similar duties to that of a press agent, promoter, booking agent, business manager (who is usually a certified public accountant), tour manager, and sometimes even a personal assistant. A music manager becomes important to managing the many different pieces that make up a career in music and vary greatly depending on the manager's ability and the musician's career path.

### Other Specialized Agency Representation
In addition to the above, there is a host of other specialized agency representation available if your child is uniquely gifted or talented, including Hosting Agents, Dance Agents, Stunt Actor Agencies, Body Part Agencies (eyes, hands, arms, legs, feet, etc.), Specialized Acts Agencies for the representation of, for example, acrobatics, celebrity look-a-likes, contortionists, mimes, puppeteers, etc., and, although not specifically relevant to your child, there are even Animal Talent Agencies in the event your dog or cat is ready to join your child for a career in Television or Film!

### Single-Category vs. Multiple-Category Agency Representation
Many Talent Agents and agencies choose to represent a particular child (or adult) actor or actress in just a single category, even where the agency represents some people in several of the above categories. Others enjoy, or even prefer, to represent child actors in multiple categories. It is common, for example, for an agency to represent someone both "theatrically" and "commercially" or for "print" and "commercials." Still others will represent your child "Across the Board," which means they will represent your child in all categories available at the agency. There are no set rules or regulations that govern this decision, but rather it is unique to each agency and its ownership. Sometimes a parent or child prefers to have separate agency representation for each category, while others prefer the simplicity and continuity of being represented by one agency, across the board. The decision is a very personal one for any parent or child, and while a detailed evaluation of this issue will be the subject of a future Blog, it is worth noting that there is nothing improper or illegal about across-the-board representation.

# CHAPTER 4

## AVOIDING SCAMS: HOW TO IDENTIFY LEGITIMATE TALENT AGENTS AND TALENT MANAGERS

*If you're going to try and hide something,*
*sooner or later people are going to find out.*

—Lou Ferrigno

From 2006 to 2008, the Better Business Bureau received approximately 1,000 complaints and 143,000 inquiries and questions related to acting and modeling scams. And that was just in Southern California alone! These scams often target child performers and their families, so it's important that you learn to protect yourself. This chapter shows you how to identify some common scams that were outlawed in California in 2010, what to do if you believe you may have already been scammed, and how to identify legitimate Talent Agents and Talent Managers.

California recently enacted a new law, the "Fee-Related Talent Services Act," to combat some of the most egregious entertainment industry scams. The Act affects all service industries related to actors and performers, including acting schools, casting workshops, and website listing services.

The law targets those people who mislead parents into thinking their children are engaging in a casting process, frequently with promises of roles on TV shows or movies, and often promising stardom. A typical scam involves charging parents exorbitant amounts of money for services such as acting classes, headshots, and industry advice and counsel. The scammers typically lure the families in by focusing on the child's dreams and selling the parents on the child's chance at Hollywood fame. The sales pitch and enticement is often so strong and so well orchestrated that even the most reasonable and brightest of parents often become victims.

The law divides the fee-related talent service industry into four distinct categories:

1.  *Advance Fee Talent Representation Services.* A Talent Agent, Talent Manager, or any other person or company is strictly prohibited from charging an "advance fee" (upfront fee) for procuring or attempting to procure an audition for employment for a role on a TV

show, a feature Film project, commercial, or modeling job, or for managing the development of an artist's career. Such services can only be charged on a commission basis (either a percentage or a flat fee), after your child has received a paying job.

2. *Talent Counseling Services.* These services are generally permitted to charge a fee to provide entertainment career evaluation and counseling, coaching, seminars, workshops or similar training to help educate you on how to get started in the entertainment business, provided certain conditions are met.

3. *Talent Training Services.* These services are generally permitted to charge a fee for lessons, coaching, seminars, workshops or similar training, such as Casting Director Workshops and Acting Schools, provided that the service complies with certain regulations.

4. *Talent Listing Services.* Talent Listing services are permitted provided they meet certain requirements. This category includes, but is not limited to, Internet-based or other online casting services, and presumably such services offered to "extras" or "background" players, or listings for auditions or employment opportunities in the Entertainment Industry, including providing the Artist with the ability to perform self-directed searches of any database or auditions, or database for Talent Agents or Talent Managers.

The "permitted" Talent Services, mentioned above, are only authorized providing the person or company enters a formal written contract with the Artist. The complete list of contract requirements can be found in Section 1703 of the California Labor Code. Here are some of the most important provisions:

- A written contract between the Talent Service and the Artist must be entered (signed and dated) before the Artist becomes obligated to pay any fee (an exception is a contract executed through the Internet, provided it is available to be downloaded and copied).

- The written contract must include the name, address, telephone number, fax number (if any), website (if any), e-mail (if any), for the Talent Service, the Talent Services representative executing the contract, and the Artist.

- The contract must provide a description of the services to be performed and when they are to be performed.

- The contract must provide a description of the duration of the contract, which may not exceed one year and may not be automatically renewed.

- The amount of the fee charged or collected and the date or dates those fees are due must be clearly stated.

- The contract must provide evidence that the Talent Service is in compliance with the applicable bonding requirement of the California Labor Commissioner, including the name of the bonding company, the bond number (if any) and a statement that the $50,000 bond was filed with the Labor Commissioner.

- A clear statement, in BOLDFACE TYPE stating, among other things, that the Talent Service is not a licensed Talent Agency, the contract is not a Talent Agency Contract, and that only licensed Talent Agents may legally procure employment.

- A provision explaining the details of the Artist's right to cancel the contract.

The California Labor Code also lists additional rules and regulations related to cancellations and refunds.

The failure by the person or company offering Talent Services to comply with these and any of the other strict contract provisions required under the law makes the contract voidable by the Artist at any time without any penalty whatsoever. If the contract does, however, comply with the law, the talent needs to move quickly to cancel a Talent Services Contract and receive a complete refund of payments made under the contract. Specifically, a person who wishes to cancel a Talent Services Contract is permitted to do so, and receive a full refund, if the cancellation takes place within ten business days from the date the artist commences using the services of the company. No specific explanation or reason is necessary other than the desire to cancel. Additionally, if cancellation takes place after the end of the ten-day cancellation period, the Artist is entitled to receive a proportional (prorata) refund. In addition, the Talent Services Contract must inform the artist that the cancellation will be acceptable if sent by mail, personal delivery, fax, or, if the contract was executed through the Internet, by

Internet. It must also provide an address to which to send the cancellation notice. Once the notice is delivered, the refund must be made within ten business days.

The law provides even more severe penalties for intentional violations. In fact, a person or company offering Talent Services can be prosecuted with criminal misdemeanors, punishable with up to a $10,000 fine, imprisonment in county jail for up to one year for each offense, or both. Likewise, failure to comply can also result in a civil lawsuit for enforcement, a restraining order against the wrongdoer, and monetary damages including the entitlement to "no less than three times the amount paid to the service" plus attorneys' fees and costs. The Los Angeles District Attorney's office has already successfully prosecuted several cases against such scam artists.

In summary, while it is always and ultimately a parent's responsibility to protect their children from scams and other predators, there are finally some very strong laws in place that can help you. If you, as a parent, grandparent, or responsible adult, suspect that you or a child you know may have been cheated by any of the service providers described above, contact an experienced entertainment attorney as soon as possible.

## IDENTIFYING LEGITIMATE TALENT AGENTS

Because Talent Agents must be licensed and bonded, doing a little bit of online research before meeting with a potential Talent Agent, and asking the following questions, will help you ensure that you are dealing with someone who is legitimate:

- Are you licensed and bonded by the California Labor Commissioner?

- Have your Talent Agency contracts and agreements been approved by the California Labor Commissioner?

- Is your fee capped at ten percent?

- Is the Talent Agency franchised with the Screen Actor's Guild (SAG), or is it a Member of the Association of Talent Agents (ATA)?

- Do you charge any advance fees or upfront costs?

- Do you require actors to go to certain photographers?

- Are your clients required to attend acting classes taught by people from the Talent Agency or by people with whom you have a financial interest?

## IDENTIFYING LEGITIMATE TALENT MANAGERS

There are a few telltale signs that will help you identify a legitimate Talent Manager in California—possibly anywhere. When choosing someone to work with your child, recognize that good Talent Managers do and don't do certain things, as follows:

- Good Talent Managers *will* advise actors on their image, resume format and content, headshots, acting classes, demo reels, websites, personal appearance and overall career direction. Will yours?

- Good Talent Managers make sure actors are accurately listed on IMDB, Actors Access, and LA Casting and that an actor's membership is current with SAG-AFTRA, and other collective guilds or unions. Will yours?

- Good Talent Managers help an actor find a talent agency when the time is right—usually as soon as possible, and work closely with the Talent Agent. Will yours?

- The *best Talent Managers* determine an actor's most marketable type and the kinds of projects for which an actor is most likely to find work. This skill is what often separates the good Talent Manager from the very best.

- Legitimate Talent Managers will *never* sell you acting classes, workshops or coaching sessions, although they will likely recommend classes, coaches, and workshops and various options for you.

- Legitimate Talent Managers will *never* refer you to classes or workshops in which they have a financial interest.

- Legitimate Talent Managers will *never* sell you photography packages, although they will very likely recommend photographers who they believe will be best for you.

- Legitimate Talent Managers will only offer you their professional guidance and services; you will only pay them based on a percentage of what you actually earn.

Most managers care very much about the lives of their client actors and can often become deeply involved with them while helping them along their career journeys. Good Talent Managers will work closely with the parents of the children and the children they represent. For this more intimate and intensive work, managers typically require longer-term contracts and sometimes, in fact often, commission percentages that exceed ten percent. These days, it is not uncommon for top managers to also be producers, and thus create the very venues through which their clients acquire employment.

As close as the client-Talent Agent relationship is, the client-Talent Manager relationship should be even closer.

# CHAPTER 5

## HOW TALENT MANAGERS JEOPARDIZE THEIR COMMISSIONS: PROCUREMENT VIOLATIONS

*We all make choices, but in the end our choices make us.*

—Ken Levine, TV Writer, Blogger

In Chapter 2, we learned that the primary legal difference between Talent Agents and Talent Managers is that only agents are allowed to "procure" work for their clients. Despite the rule, the realities of Hollywood are that the process of getting auditions can be fluid. Managers, acting in good faith, want to help their clients and are often tempted to cross the line and actively seek auditions. In fact, this happens fairly often, both in connection with entertainment kids and adult talent.

Arsenio Hall, Pamela Anderson, and Rosa Blasi are just a few of the celebrities who have been involved in lawsuits with their Talent Managers. Each accused his/her manager of unlawfully infringing on an agent's exclusive right to procure work. Although these lawsuits involved adult stars, the procurement rules also apply to Hollywood Kids. Because these lawsuits can be time-consuming, expensive, and distracting, it's important that you understand the basics of what unlawful procurement involves.

The case of Rosa Blasi, Star of the Lifetime television series *Strong Medicine*, is instructive. In 1998, when she was twenty-six years old,

Rosa Blasi entered into a verbal contract with Marathon Entertainment, Inc. to serve as Blasi's personal manager. [1] Marathon was to advise Blasi and promote her career; in exchange, Blasi was to pay Marathon fifteen percent of her earnings from entertainment employment obtained during the course of the contract. During the ensuing three years, Blasi's professional appearances included a role in a Film, *Noriega: God's Favorite*, and a lead role as Dr. Luisa Delgado on *Strong Medicine*, which was co-executive produced by Whoopi Goldberg.

Marathon sued Blasi, accusing her of breaking her promise to pay Marathon its fifteen percent commission from her *Strong Medicine* employment contract. According to Marathon, in the summer of 2001, she unilaterally reduced payments to ten percent. Later that year, she allegedly ceased payment altogether and terminated her Marathon contract, stating that her licensed Talent Agent, John Kelly, who had served as her agent throughout the term of the management contract with Marathon, was going to become her new personal manager.

Marathon accused Blasi of breaking the oral contract and of committing certain unfair business practices. Marathon claimed that one of their principals, Rick Siegal, had provided Blasi with lawful personal manager services, including paying for her home, travel expenses, and advising her on her career. Marathon sought a court order requiring Blasi to pay her unpaid *Strong Medicine* commissions.

In response, Blasi filed a complaint arguing that Marathon had violated the *Talent Agencies Act* (TAA) by engaging in unlawful "procurement" activities. The TAA, which regulates Talent Agents, has as its primary goal, protecting all artists, including actors and actresses, from exploitation. Because of its protective purpose, agents and managers must closely follow its provisions.

The California Labor Commissioner, who, unless the parties otherwise agree, has the authority to resolve disputes between actors and Talent Agents and Talent Managers. Traditionally, the Commission used a broad definition to determine when managers engage in unlawful procurement practices. For example, in a case involving a dispute between late night TV host Arsenio Hall and his Talent Manager, the commissioner defined procurement as involving more than soliciting

---

[1] If you are wondering whether it's a good idea to enter into a talent management agreement that isn't in writing, it isn't. See Chapter 10 for more about the importance of written contracts.

contracts for the actor; it includes negotiating contracts, and "means either to secure employment or to bring about employment or cause employment to occur."

The Labor Commission has also ruled that a Talent Manager unlawfully procures employment by initiating or attending meetings with executives in order to advertise the artist's talent and make them aware of the talent's availability. Likewise, a case involving actress Pamela Anderson held that a manager violated the Act simply by having discussions with producers or casting directors in an attempt to obtain her auditions.

Using the Commission's broad definition of procurement may severely penalize managers for a wide range of procurement-related conduct. The traditional rule was extremely harsh; it held that a single act of unlawful procurement automatically voided the manager's contract— entirely. The contract was treated as if it never existed in the first place, and the manager could be required to reimburse money previously earned under the contract! Voiding the contract not only nullifies the manager's right to receive commissions under the contract; it also gives actors the right to seek reimbursement of commissions earned during the year prior to the filing of the complaint against the manager.

That's what Blasi sought when she filed her complaint with the California Labor Commission. She argued that Marathon had engaged in unlawful procurement activities and that they should therefore be barred from collecting any unpaid *Strong Medicine* commissions. Moreover, Blasi asked the Commission to order the Talent Manager to return all commissions that he had received from Blasi during the previous year.

The dispute between Blasi and Marathon eventually reached the California Supreme Court. In January 2008, the California Supreme Court decided that *"collateral" acts of unlawful procurement no longer automatically void the manager's entire agreement*. Instead, the Labor Commissioner or trial judge has the discretion to decide if the manager is entitled to some compensation even if incidental acts of unlawful procurement took place.

However, even under the new rule, managers may still be required to reimburse a year's commissions or more if they infringe on the agent's job of procuring work. This is an important issue and an important distinction between Talent Agents and Talent Managers. It affects the language that appears in their respective contracts and how Talent

Managers operate as professionals.

Although Rosa Blasi was an adult when she entered into her agreement with her Talent Manager, the procurement rules also apply to children in entertainment. Thus, one should continue to monitor how agents and managers handle auditions and engage in related procurement activities because the bottom line is that only agents are authorized to procure work for your children. Although a single act of procurement by a Talent Manager no longer automatically invalidates the entire contract with the manager, it's still important for parents and guardians of children in Hollywood to appreciate this distinction *before* you sign a contract with either a Talent Manager or a Talent Agent.

In addition, and as explained in more detail in the next chapter, you can do something to address the procurement violation problem after you have signed contracts with both a Talent Agent and a Talent Manager.

# CHAPTER 6

## "SAFE HARBOR" AUTHORIZATION AND REQUEST

*A ship is safe in harbor, but that's not what ships are for.*

—William Shedd

A little-known law allows a Talent Manager to legally procure employment for an actor. Although the rule of law has its limitations, and is narrowly interpreted, this well-kept secret gives your child's Talent Manager (or any *unlicensed* talent representative) a "safe harbor" to engage in certain forms of procurement normally only authorized for Talent Agents. Specifically, if the Talent Manager obtains a "safe harbor" authorization from your child's Talent Agent, the manager can legally *negotiate* employment agreements for your child. In short, under this rule of law, if the Talent Agent wants, he can ask for the Talent Manager's assistance to essentially "act as a Talent Agent" in certain limited situations.

The relevant provision of the California *Labor Code* authorizing this "safe harbor" is found in the *Talent Agencies Act* at *Labor Code* §1700.44(d). It says that a Talent Manager can work in conjunction with, and at the request of, a licensed Talent Agent.

> *(d) It is not unlawful for a person or corporation which is not licensed pursuant to this chapter (e.g., a Talent Manager) to act in conjunction with, and at the request of, a licensed talent agency in the negotiation of an employment contract.*

The only way for this rule of law to take legal effect for the Talent Manager is if the Talent Agent requests (asks) the manager for his or her assistance *negotiating* a TV, Film, commercials or other employment contract. The request by the Talent Agent should be clear and unequivocal and, therefore, is best conveyed in writing.

On a practical level, this means a licensed Talent Agent can provide your Talent Manager with a legal, "safe harbor" letter. With letter in hand, your Talent Manager may work harder or feel more involved in the outcome of your child's career. The Talent Manager has nothing to lose from this request and much to gain. If a proper "safe harbor" letter is in place, everyone wins if the manager helps to negotiate a contract that ultimately results in employment or in better contract terms for your child. Sophisticated and experienced Talent Managers often add language to their management contract that requires an actor and parents to help obtain a "safe harbor" letter from the Talent Agent. This is an example of language you might see:

> *Both Parent and Artist shall encourage, assist and cooperate with manager's efforts in obtaining a Safe Harbor Letter(s) from Artist's licensed Talent Agent(s) so that Manager may assist in the procurement of employment, development of actor's career and with negotiations being conducted by Artist's Talent Agent.*

Whether or not the provision appears in the talent management agreement is not really the issue. What matters most for the Talent Manager is that he does get this permission before undertaking procurement activities.

While it is not your obligation as a parent to educate your child's Talent Agent or Talent Manager of the limitations of a "safe harbor" request, here are some brief descriptions so you are personally knowledgeable on the subject. First, "safe harbor" requests are generally not applicable to all types of procurement activity, but rather have most often been limited to the *negotiation of employment contracts*. More so, the rule has generally been limited to situations *where the employment has already been procured (obtained) by the Talent Agent*, which means the "safe harbor" request does not generally authorize the Talent Manager to "seek" or "solicit" employment. Third, the "safe harbor" typically only applies when the Talent Manager is *working in conjunction with* the licensed Talent Agent, as compared to the Talent Manager who obtains a "safe harbor" and tries to work on his own thereafter. Fourth, the Labor Commissioner has generally found that any "safe harbor" request must be project-specific, meaning that "blanket requests" are generally not permitted.

Also, as a parent, keep in mind that some Talent Agents will graciously and willingly provide a Talent Manager with a "safe harbor" letter, whereas some Talent Agents or agencies have a strict policy against them. Whatever position your agent or agency takes on this issue is fair and reasonable, and I would strongly suggest that you respect it and accept it.

Regardless of the limitations discussed above, "safe harbor" requests do and will continue to benefit Talent Managers who follow the rules regarding them. And when they are issued, they can help your Talent Manager to further your child's career. Also, regardless of the wording of the "safe harbor" letter, it should be prepared on your agent's letterhead and addressed to your child's Talent Manager. A personalized formal email that is very specific and well written by the Talent Agent and sent to the Talent Manager may also suffice. However transmitted, the letter should be structured essentially as follows:

> *Dear (manager's name):*
>
> *We are aware that you are the Talent Manager for (child's full name).*
>
> *Pursuant to Labor Code 1700.44 (d), we are requesting your assistance with our negotiation of (child's name) potential employment contract for acting services with (employer's name) regarding (project name).*
>
> *Thank you for your assistance with this important matter.*
>
> *Agent's Signature*

In summary, if a Talent Manager wants a "safe harbor," it is in your and your child's interest to help him get it by encouraging, or at least asking, your Talent Agent to issue one. Most Talent Managers will feel more appreciated and protected knowing you're watching out for their interests as they engage in what would otherwise be considered (without the "safe harbor" letter) unauthorized procurement activity. This, in turn, will likely foster a stronger working relationship for all of you and may very well motivate the manager to work harder for your child.

# CHAPTER 7

## WHAT A TALENT MANAGER WON'T DO: EXCLUDED SERVICES

*You are what you do, not what you say you'll do.*

—Carl Jung, Swiss Psychiatrist

Many talent management contracts contain a provision entitled "Excluded Services," where the Talent Manager tells you what they will and won't do for you and your child.

The contract will likely include a description of those roles and obligations that the manager will not do for your child. In many cases, this is where the Talent Manager explains that:

- You and the manager are not forming a business partnership or joint venture, and your child is not an employee of the manager.

  Sample language: *This Agreement does not form a partnership or joint venture agreement between Artist or Parent and Manager. Manager is strictly in an independent contractor relationship with Artist and Parent.*

- This is not an exclusive arrangement and they are free to represent others, including other kids who may compete for roles and auditions with your child.

  Sample language: *Manager's services are not exclusive to Artist and Parent, and Artist and Parent are aware that Manager has other clients for whom Manager performs similar services.*

- Manager is not a licensed Talent Agent.

  Sample language: *Manager is not licensed as a Talent Agent or talent agency or employment agency (as defined in Labor Code §1700.4 or any other applicable law) and Manager has made no such representation to Artist or Parent to the contrary. Nevertheless, Manager may assist a licensed Talent Agent in procuring or negotiating employment for Artist when requested to do so by Artist's Talent Agent, as authorized by California Labor Code §1700.44(d). Otherwise, Manager will not take any action to procure employment for Artist. Manager has made no claim that Manager will, nor has Manager any obligation to, solicit, procure and/or negotiate employment for Artist. Any other use of the word agent hereinafter is used in the generic and legal sense and does not refer to a "Talent Agent" unless specifically stated.* [2]

- Many managers also add an additional paragraph making it clear they're not business managers, attorneys or tax advisors.

  Sample language: *Manager is not an acting coach, accountant, business manager, entertainment attorney, photographer, publicist, or tax advisor. Manager is not obligated to provide services associated with those professions. However, Manager can assist Artist and Parent in developing relationships with experts in those areas.*

Managers include language about Excluded Services to protect themselves legally. There is nothing wrong with that, and this language is generally not problematic. There is no reason to be alarmed by this language, so long as it accurately reflects what you and the manager agreed upon.

Often language in the contract describes the extent of the work they will perform on behalf of your child. This language has, over time, become more and more detailed.

If you are looking at a contract that hasn't been modified in some time, you may see the following language:

Sample language: *Manager will "devote reasonable time and attention to the development and advancement of the Artist's career."*

The key phrase is "reasonable time and attention." Because this is a business arrangement, "reasonable" means "commercially reasonable." Thus, for example, I offer a word of caution: if your child is sent to ten auditions and none of them pan out, it might be commercially reasonable for your manager to devote less time to your child's career.

Today, you are more likely to see a much more detailed description

---

[2] As is discussed in the next chapter, a small minority of managers do intend to simultaneously act as your child's manager and agent.

of the Talent Manager's responsibilities, such as:

Sample language: *Manager agrees to perform the following services for Artist and Parent during the term of this Agreement:*

> *a) To advise and counsel Artist and Parent on the selection, engagement and discharge of other entertainment industry professionals for Artist, such as, but not limited to, acting coaches, Talent Agents, business managers, entertainment attorneys, photographers, publicists, or tax advisors for the development of a support team as requested by Artist or as deemed necessary by Manager;*

> *b) To use reasonable and good faith efforts to promote, develop and advance Artist's professional career and to advise and counsel Artist and Parent with respect to all phases of the entertainment industry relating to Artist;*

> *c) To advise and counsel Artist and Parent with respect to the general practices of the entertainment industry and as specifically related to Artist;*

> *d) To advise and counsel Artist and Parent with respect to promoting Artist's career;*

> *e) To advise and counsel Artist and Parent as to the proper formats and best places to present Artist's talents and skills, resume and biographical information to industry professionals;*

> *f) To advise and counsel Artist and Parent with respect to the benefits, responsibilities, and obligations in matters relating specifically to children and young performers in the entertainment industry, including work permits and unions and/or Guilds (e.g. SAG-AFTRA);*

> *g) To advise and counsel Artist and Parent as to the proper style, mood, setting and characterization needed to present Artist's talents and skills pertaining to Artist's endeavors and goals in the entertainment industry;*

> *h) To advise and counsel Artist and Parent with respect to compensation, income and earnings, including privileges and other amenities that Artist is entitled to receive or may be eligible for in exchange for his or her professional services;*

*i) To collaborate with, and at the request of, a licensed Talent Agent in procuring employment for Artist to the extent expressly permitted by law under California Labor Code § 1700.44 (d).*

# CHAPTER 8

## DO YOU NEED A TALENT AGENT, TALENT MANAGER, OR BOTH?

*Choices are the hinges of destiny.*

—Pythagoras

"Which is best for my child—a Talent Agent or a Talent Manager, and do I need both?"

When the parents of Hollywood kids get together, this question invariably comes up. It's one of those questions where it's easy to have an opinion and to hear contradictory advice. Wherein some say you should get a Talent Agent first; others are just as sincere in advocating on behalf of Talent Managers. It's no wonder that parents and others who are relatively new to the scene are confused and anxious; it feels like such an important decision—one that could potentially derail a child's ability to get noticed and have a chance at success in Hollywood.

Before addressing the "Talent Agent or Talent Manager" question, I'll cue you in on a secret: The answer to this question is often less important than many parents, Talent Agents, and Talent Managers realize. Here's why. Most children who, like Craig Traylor, "want to be on TV," at most go to a few auditions before trying something else. The biggest challenge, therefore, for people (children and adults) who want to make it in Hollywood is making enough initial progress so that they stick with it. In other words, the hardest part is getting some kind of traction at the beginning; the primary obstacle is getting enough positive attention to get in front of the camera (or on stage).

Because both Talent Agents and Talent Managers can be invaluable in helping your child get a good start, finding a good agent or manager who works well with your child and tries hard to get him/ her noticed is, *at the very beginning*, more important than whether they are either a Talent Agent or a Talent Manager. Likewise, working well with that person, whether they are a Talent Agent or a Talent Manager, is often more important than whether your child *first* works with an agent or a manager.[3]

That said, ultimately, your child *needs* an agent because, as you now know, only agents can lawfully procure work. Your child needs an agent to get auditions. Everyone needs an agent. But if you can first only establish a good working relationship with a Talent Manager, that is much better than going it alone. And, as was discussed in Chapter 2, a good Talent Manager will help you find a Talent Agent.

Finally, we briefly address the question, set forth below, as to whether one person can be both your child's Talent Agent *and* Talent Manager.

## WHEN YOUR MANAGER TELLS YOU
## THEY ARE ALSO A TALENT AGENT

In recent years, a handful of Talent Managers have chosen to take the position that they are both Talent Managers *and* Talent Agents. Why would a Talent Manager want to also be an agent? The answer is simple: so that they can also legally procure work and get paid commissions for doing so. As was discussed in Chapters 2 and 5, only Talent Agents may lawfully procure work for their clients. That means that in California a Talent Manager can't do things like seek or find employment for the talent, formally submit to *Breakdown Services,* make pitch calls to casting directors, directors or producers, negotiate deal points, negotiate contract terms, or even, most significantly, officially book the project. All of these activities potentially violate the *Talent Agencies Act.* When a manager violates this law, he can, under certain circumstances, lose his commission. Thus, when a Talent Manager takes the position that they are both a Talent Manager and a Talent Agent and undertake the effort to become a licensed Talent Agent, they do so (if not exclusively) to avoid being charged with illegal activity and hope to avoid the potential consequences of that activity.

Whether a Talent Manager legally can also act as your Talent Agent isn't entirely clear under California law. From the parents' point of view, however, the most important thing is to know whether the manager you are interviewing also wants to be your child's agent. This doesn't happen often, but if it does, you need to know in advance about

---

[3] Knowing what it means to work well with a Talent Agent or Talent Manager, and what kind of behavior generally doesn't work, is so important that Part III of this book is devoted to it.

this dual status.

Fortunately, the contract that you are given by the Talent Manager will generally make clear if they are also seeking to be the Talent Agent.

A typical dual representation provision reads like this:

> *Talent Manager is licensed by the State of California to solicit, procure and negotiate employment for Artist pursuant to the provisions of the California Talent Agencies Act. Manager shall, therefore, use reasonable efforts to procure employment for Artist in the areas of entertainment covered by this agreement. In addition to Talent Manager herein, Artist may find it advisable to have a Talent Agent to solicit and procure employment. If Artist retains or engages a separate Talent Agent, Artist is responsible for any commissions, costs or other compensation payable to Talent Agent. Artist agrees to consult with Talent Manager concerning the selection and retention of a Talent Agent and will instruct any and all of Artist's Talent Agents to communicate with Talent Manager and coordinate with Talent Manager in all aspects of Artist's career.*

This kind of provision may very well be a good thing for Talent Managers to do. Anyone who seeks to take on a dual role as a manager and an agent assumes a certain amount of legal risk because this arrangement has not yet been *formally* approved by the California legislature or the courts. Thus, in the rare case in which you come across someone wanting to act as both Talent Agent and Talent Manager, I suggest you seek legal advice from an experienced entertainment lawyer.

From a parent's point of view, agreeing to work with someone who is going to be your child's agent and manager means that you are putting more of your eggs in one basket. There is nothing inherently wrong with that. On the one hand, this kind of arrangement can be more efficient and effective than having a separate manager and agent. By going down this road, you largely eliminate the chances that the agent and manager won't get along or that they will get involved in turf battles.

On the other hand, having one person act as both Talent Agent and Talent Manager means that it is even more important than usual to select the right person for these roles. You and your child must like and trust this individual. In addition, it is critical that this person has the necessary connections to get your child auditions while simultaneously following industry trends and managing your child's career. Is this too much to ask of one person? The decision is yours, but you need to ask hard questions about the commitment and resources of anyone who wants to act as both Talent Agent and Talent Manager.

This, therefore, takes us back to where this chapter started. Whether you work first with a Talent Agent, or a Talent Manager, and whether you use two separate people to fill these roles over time, or have the same person act as your child's agent and manager, protecting yourself and your child comes down to working with experienced and professional people whom:

- You like and trust;

- Have the necessary connections to help your child along his/her journey;

- Will work hard and diligently on your child's behalf; and

- Will communicate often and honestly with you about what they are doing.

# CHAPTER 9
## WHAT ENTERTAINMENT LAWYERS DO TO PROTECT
## CHILDREN IN HOLLYWOOD

*Anybody who thinks talk is cheap should get*
*some legal advice.*

—Franklin P. Jones, American Journalist and Humorist

Whether you are working with a Talent Manager or a Talent Agent, or both, your team is not quite complete. You will also need, at some point, an entertainment lawyer. This chapter explains why, what kind of lawyer you need, when to hire one, how the right lawyer can help you and your child, and how lawyers get paid.

## WHY YOU NEED AN ENTERTAINMENT LAWYER

The short answer is this: You need an entertainment lawyer because the Film studios, TV producers, and advertising agencies always have their best attorneys negotiate the bigger, more lucrative deals. Their job is to get the best deal possible for their employers, not your child. Most of the time, the contracts that you are asked to sign were drafted by lawyers representing the person or company who wants you to sign that contract. You need to protect yourself and often can get a better deal when the other side knows you have your own attorney. Sometimes the problem with the contracts isn't what's in them; it's what's not there. Experienced lawyers can tell you the significance of what's there, and the importance of what's missing. That's very hard for you to know on your own, which is why most people who try to negotiate by themselves are likely to be tragically out-gunned.

Hiring a lawyer is particularly important in projects involving children, since there are special laws that uniquely apply to any contract involving a minor. Additionally, parents must understand any potential liability or responsibility they may bear—all of which depends on the specific language of the contract.

## What Kind of Entertainment Attorney Do You Need?

Notice that this question did not say, "What kind of lawyer do you need?" That's easy. You should focus on finding an attorney who practices exclusively in Entertainment Law, or who has a practice that emphasizes work in this area. In particular, focus on lawyers who are experienced in representing children in the entertainment industry. Most lawyers learn what they know on the job. Experience matters and you want someone who already has worked representing children in Hollywood. You should, therefore, avoid hiring, for example, your family probate attorney (aka "wills and trusts" attorney), real estate attorney or general practitioner for anything related to the entertainment industry, and, in particular, anything related to representing children in entertainment. Well-intentioned family and friends who are not entertainment attorneys can inadvertently cause more harm than good by trying to help someone save a little money or work on an entertainment deal that really needs entertainment expertise.

Generally speaking, entertainment lawyers come in two flavors. You will find that even attorneys in the entertainment industry generally define themselves as either "transactional attorneys" or "litigation attorneys." Transactional attorneys deal with contract negotiations, preparation of contracts, closing television, Film, or production deals, and related issues. Litigation attorneys, by contrast, deal with actual and threatened lawsuits and other disputes. Litigation attorneys may, for example, help you informally fix deals that went bad, or help you collect money that you feel is owed to you or your child, or protect you from unfair demands for your child to violate Screen Actors' Guild rules or other rules, or demands for you or your child to pay someone else.

Litigation doesn't just involve lawsuits in a court. It may also include disputes before the California Labor Commissioner, who governs all claims related to violations of the Talent Agency Act. Litigation includes mediation of disputes, arbitrations, and, of course, can include disputes before a judge or jury in the courthouse. Some attorneys do one or the other: transactional or litigation—some do both, so from your perspective the most important thing is to "know to whom you're talking" when you're talking to an entertainment attorney. The difference between the two is significant, so if you need a transactional attorney, make sure you select one, and if you need a litigation attorney, be sure you hire someone comfortable and experienced in litigation.

## WHEN DO I NEED AN ATTORNEY?

Most of the deals negotiated in Hollywood unfold quickly, and often impose seemingly unrealistic demands on actors. For example, a studio that informs your child's Talent Agent that they are interested in him or her for a Recurring or Series Regular role on a television program will often want you to sign off on the contract, (typically called a "Test Option Agreement") within 48 hours. Often there is a spoken or implied threat that if you don't act quickly, the producer or production company will move on to another actor, which means that your child's dream job could evaporate before your very eyes if you don't meet their deadlines.

So what do you do? Line up an experienced entertainment lawyer in advance. While calling a lawyer at the last minute is almost always better than trying to negotiate on your own and over the years I have received many last-minute calls—the better approach by far is to interview and select an entertainment lawyer ahead of time. This allows you to find someone you feel comfortable with, and who knows you, your child, and potentially your Talent Agent and Talent Manager, too. With this team in place, when the time comes to close a deal, you can move quickly and effectively.

The best time to form a relationship with an attorney is when you anticipate forming a relationship with a Talent Agent or Talent Manager, or when your child is offered his or her very first job, but before you sign anything. You, as the parent, may have negotiated that first job yourself. That's not uncommon, but nothing is official until you and your child sign the contract. That's a good time to get your lawyer involved.

In their book, *All You Need to Know about the Movie and TV Business*, Gail Resnick and Scott Trost list three reasons for hiring a lawyer early in the process:

- "First, you should get in the habit of understanding all the ramifications of every relationship you enter." A lawyer is well positioned to help you understand those ramifications.

- Second, "[e]ven the most standard agreements leave room for negotiation." Thus, for example, "maybe that [talent] manager will not budge from demanding 15% of all the money you earn until they put you in the grave, but what about that 'power of attorney' clause? Perhaps he will back off from including an unlimited 'power of attorney' clause. If you don't know what a 'power of attorney' clause is, that's all the more reason to be sitting down with your trusted attorney. A good attorney can't save you from signing away your soul, but he can perhaps help you limit some of the more onerous terms in these agreements."

- Third, "if your career goes the way you dream it will, you will have the need for an attorney for many years to come. Learning to work with one early in your career—when less is at stake—gives you the chance to test the waters and find the right match."

## For What Kinds of Deals are Lawyers Most Useful?

The bigger the role, the more important it is to hire an experienced entertainment lawyer. As careers develop and roles grow from a Day Player (Co-Star), to Guest Star, to Recurring Roles and eventually to Series Regular roles on episodic television, or from non-union PSAs, Industrials or local commercials to national campaigns, or from small independent Films to Major Motion Pictures, the amount of money at stake becomes larger and larger and the legal issues become more complicated. Likewise, the other terms of the contract, which are referred to as "deal points," become more negotiable. Chapter 21 discusses these deal points in great detail. But for now, recognize that parent and child should not put themselves at a disadvantage to the producers and production companies who virtually always have experienced entertainment attorneys handling their side of the negotiations.

Moreover, while I am a big fan of Talent Agents and Talent Managers, and, in fact, was a Talent Agent for many years and a Talent Manager for several more, neither a Talent Agent nor a Talent Manager is a substitute for an entertainment lawyer. Under the law, Talent Agents can negotiate deals, but most are not equipped to do so with the same expertise as an entertainment lawyer. Talent Managers are not even permitted by law to do so, which means that you must be very cautious in encouraging your Talent Manager to "play lawyer" when the stakes are so important to your child's long-term career.

I know that some Talent Agents and Talent Managers and even some well-intentioned family and friends might believe that lawyers can so overly nit-pick at the language of a contract that the process becomes counterproductive at best or a nightmare at worst. Some believe that involving lawyers will "kill the deal" if you don't watch over them. Personally, that is not my experience in the real world—especially in dealing with children in entertainment. A good entertainment lawyer will work hard to protect you while, at the same time, understanding that, most of the time, actors and other performers want to get deals finalized. You should, therefore, take the time to find an experienced entertainment lawyer in advance—one you like, one whom you work well with, one whom you relate to, and one who understands your goals and what's important to you when it comes to booking projects and closing deals.

## WHAT ARE THE BENEFITS OF HIRING A LAWYER IF SOMETHING GOES WRONG?

It's even more important and helpful to hire a lawyer for a potential or threatened lawsuit, or other entertainment-related dispute. By now you know that Hollywood is a relationship-oriented business. Relationships involve communication, and communication is subject to being misunderstood. Throw in large amounts of money and sizeable egos. Is it any wonder, therefore, that the entertainment business sees more than its fair share of disputes and lawsuits?

Most of these disagreements involve money and miscommunications or differences of opinion about what was said or promised. For example, the actor, Talent Agent, or Talent Manager may believe that they didn't get what they were owed on a project. It can also be the Film studio or union which claims that some rule, regulation, or law was broken. Another common dispute involves co-producers or business partners which disagree over

### CASE STUDY

*While most Talent Agents and Talent Managers will help you understand their contracts for representation, others in the industry are not so generous. In one extreme example, my client, a young and very talented girl, was offered the lead role on a major children's television series. When the family was told about the offer for the role, you can just imagine how excited they all were, that is, until the long and detailed contract arrived with an email cover letter that gave her family 22 minutes to read and sign the contract. Like most families at that time, they had not pre-screened an entertainment attorney who was prepared to take immediate action. Instead, they did the best they could with excitement and enthusiasm winning out over careful scrutiny and understanding of the contract. Several years later, when serious problems left them no alternative but to file a lawsuit, you can also imagine how much they wished they had been better prepared up front.*

what their joint venture involved, and how to split the money. In such an environment, lawsuits and threatened lawsuits are more common than in most businesses. That is why an entertainment lawyer with experience in litigation is indispensable, especially as your child works on bigger and bigger projects.

There are three especially important advantages to hiring an entertainment lawyer in connection with a potential or actual dispute. First, you can speak to your lawyer and be virtually assured that it will remain confidential. As long as you are not trying to use your lawyer to commit some future crime or commit a fraud, the law in California and throughout the United States protects communications between lawyers and their clients from being disclosed. The lawyer can't be forced to divulge what you say to him or her. This is especially important if you have concerns about talking over an issue or problem with someone you normally would trust, such as the Talent Manager, Talent Agent, or other non-lawyer. If you are involved in a lawsuit, you may be forced to disclose what you said to a Talent Agent, Talent Manager, producer, director, casting director or other non-lawyer. Your conversations with your lawyer are, by contrast, protected from disclosure. Other than in the rarest of exceptions, they will stay secret. Thus, you can get professional advice and guidance without having to worry about sharing information that you would prefer to keep confidential.

Second, if initial attempts to resolve the dispute fail, a lawyer working on your behalf in a lawsuit has the authority to force someone else to turn over documents and make statements under oath. This authority, of course, isn't absolute. A judge can overrule and limit the attorney's power, but in a vast majority of cases, when a lawsuit is filed in the entertainment business, some kind of exchange of documents, data, and sworn witness statements takes place. Thus, if you or your child desired to receive or examine certain documents or look at certain information, a lawsuit may be the only effective way to gain access to that information. By law, a Talent Agent or Talent Manager lacks the power to require someone to provide information. You can seek this information by filing a lawsuit yourself, but you will likely be much more successful if you are working with a lawyer.

Third, and perhaps most importantly, a lawyer can help prevent disputes and resolves disputes more quickly. This may seem counterintuitive, but a good entertainment lawyer will help you avoid disputes. I do so every single month. Hiring an experienced entertainment attorney tends to reduce the perceived vulnerability of parents and their children. In other words, when the other side knows you are represented by someone whom they know and respect, they tend to be more cooperative and play fewer games. In fact, deterring the other side from trying to hide things from you or take advantage of your relative inexperience is often the biggest benefit I bring to my clients, both in contract negotiations and in litigation.

## WHAT DOES AN ENTERTAINMENT LAWYER COST?

Some parents of children in the entertainment business are understandably concerned about the fees and costs that come with hiring an attorney. It has been my experience that more money and time, as well as emotional and negative energy, has been spent undoing bad deals that were never pre-approved or negotiated by an attorney, than the time, money, and negative emotion ever spent "preventively" in doing it the right way up front, the first time. Also, the issue of attorneys' fees and costs, if contemplated in advance, instead of scrambling when the deal is about to close, can be handled in a way that works for you.

Attorneys charge fees in different ways, depending on a variety of circumstances. Some entertainment attorneys charge by the hour, requiring an initial retainer (deposit) against which the hourly rate is deducted. Hourly rates vary dramatically, with larger firms generally having more strict guidelines and requirements on the hourly rate charged by an attorney in the office, how the hourly rates are charged, and the amount of the initial deposit. Smaller law firms and solo practitioners generally have more flexibility in determining the hourly rate charged, and how the hourly rates are calculated, and in accepting a retainer that works for you.

Some entertainment attorneys charge, for certain projects, flat-rate fees, where the accomplishment of certain specified work (e.g., the preparation of the contract, the review and negotiation of a contract, etc.) is promised for a one-time guaranteed flat fee. This approach allows people to know exactly where they stand right from the start, and there is no concern of "hidden fees" or other surprises when a client receives an invoice.

Some entertainment attorneys are willing to charge in a way similar to the way your Talent Agent or Talent Manager charges, by accepting a percentage of your child's gross earnings—with the percentage usually charged at not greater than 5% of gross income. This latter example is usually only seen when it is fairly predictable that your child is working regularly.

As you can see, when it comes to hiring an entertainment lawyer, a little homework will potentially give you options and allow you to negotiate and make arrangements that work best for you and your attorney. In my office, I often offer potential clients two or three different options as to how we might work together—an hourly rate, a flat fee structure, or a percentage against gross earnings—and have found that all of my clients appreciate having the choice of deciding what works best for them. I've also found, to my surprise, that people often choose options that I might not expect when I offer options on the fee structure.

## Where do You Find an Experienced Entertainment Lawyer?

In trying to decide on a good entertainment lawyer for your child, ask friends who have had good experiences with an entertainment attorney for a referral. If that doesn't work out, contact the Beverly Hills Bar Association or the Los Angeles County Bar Association, but be sure to specify that you are looking for an attorney who specializes in Entertainment Law, and if this has to do with your child, someone who has experience and expertise representing children in the entertainment business. This is because television, Film and commercial campaign projects involving children are far different from those strictly involving adults, as projects involving children deal with a special set of rules, regulations and laws.

In short, when it comes to hiring an entertainment lawyer, do it up front, do it early and give yourself some choices and options, but most of all, feel assured that the attorney whom you hire is someone with whom you can communicate openly with at any time, and in a way that makes sense to you. When you hang up the phone or walk out of the office, ask yourself if the conversation was so filled with legal jargon that you are more confused than informed, or whether you feel more knowledgeable and comfortable than when you began. Beyond the references from friends, be sure to get suggestions from someone with a reputation for honesty and who has integrity, and be sure to ask yourself if, at a gut level, you trust the attorney.

# SUMMARY OF PART I

## HOW TALENT AGENTS, TALENT MANAGERS, AND ENTERTAINMENT LAWYERS SHAPE THE CAREERS OF HOLLYWOOD KIDS

If you want to protect your entertainment kids, you need to understand the practical and legal difference between Talent Agents and managers and the role of the entertainment attorney:

- Only Talent Agents are allowed by law to procure work.

- Talent Managers can jeopardize their right to receive commissions if they unlawfully procure work, but this happens fairly often and can result in lawsuits.

- Although Talent Agents can and do negotiate the basic terms of the contract, the more significant the role and the more money involved, the more important and useful it is to use an entertainment lawyer.

- Entertainment lawyers are indispensable if you are involved in a potential or actual dispute with a Talent Agent, manager, producer, or studio about compensation or whether you and your child have met your obligations under a contract.

- Always remember that "show business," for all else it may also be, is ultimately a business. It may be fun and potentially lucrative, but it is still a business and should be treated as one.

# PART II

*What's What in Hollywood:*
*The Unspoken Rules*

# PART II

## WHAT'S WHAT IN HOLLYWOOD: THE UNSPOKEN RULES

Now that you know about Talent Managers, Talent Agents, and entertainment lawyers—the major players who help shape a child and his career—you need to understand some of the basic rules that govern how these and other Hollywood insiders act and interact with each other.

This is not a discussion of laws, which will be explained later. This is a discussion of the equally important unspoken rules. It's not that Hollywood insiders think that they are working under a specific set of rules. If you pulled them aside and asked, "Hey, what are the rules?" they wouldn't know what you were talking about. These "Rules" aren't written down anywhere; nor are Talent Agents, Talent Managers and entertainment lawyers trying to keep them a secret.

These "Rules" developed differently. Over time, insiders in Hollywood established certain ways of dealing with each other. These rules aren't always logical. They are more like an undisclosed language that insiders know and learn. When insiders meet someone new, they judge that person in part on whether, and to what extent, they seem to understand how Hollywood operates.

In other words, the rules aren't a secret, but you are judged by whether you know them, and you can be penalized if it's perceived that you don't know them. That is why it's important to know these rules and act accordingly. Specifically, knowing these rules will help you navigate the entertainment business more smoothly and, more importantly, will help parents protect their kids.

The rest of the book is full of details of what to do in specific situations that come up for parents and their children, and the legal significance of those situations. Before delving into these details, such as specific elements of contracts with Talent Managers, please take the time to understand the following Hollywood Rules.

Part II includes the following chapters:

- If It's Important, Get It in Writing
- Children Are Different
- Everything Is Negotiable
- Informed Consent

*A verbal contract isn't worth the paper it is written on.*

—Sam Goldwyn, Founding Executive
Metro-Goldwyn-Mayer (MGM) Studios

The legendary Sam Goldwyn's tongue-in-cheek comment may actually have been more accurate than even he realized—if, that is, he was talking about contracts with children. In reality, there are many widespread misconceptions about what it takes to form a legally binding contract.

In California, the law generally recognizes both verbal and written contracts. Technically, the California legislature calls a verbal contract an oral contract, but since both phrases mean the same thing, I will use the terms interchangeably.

Every industry has its own culture or way of doing things. People in the entertainment business tend to be a bit more free-wheeling than in many other industries. Perhaps this is because Hollywood is full of so many people who are creative and are less inclined to focus on getting certain details in writing. Whatever the reason, a surprising number of agreements in Hollywood, even those involving substantial amounts of money, are handled on a handshake basis.

Thus, I have often sat with people who have "handshake contracts," "verbal understandings," or at best a two-page deal memorandum rather than appropriate written contracts with their Talent Managers, Talent Agents, writing partners, co-producers and others with whom they have an ongoing business relationship. If someone does not have a signed, written contract, what they may still very well have, and likely do have, is a verbal contract, that is to say, at least among adults.

While these handshake agreements are mostly intended to be very noble, the question of whether they are binding can very often present serious legal issues that result in lawsuits. Here's why. Although a verbal contract among adults can be binding in California, proving exactly what the agreement was is much harder in the absence of a written document. You must often rely upon memories of conversations,

## CASE STUDY

*Not long ago I represented a very well-known Hollywood Talent Manager in a case involving a dispute between the manager and a well-known Series Regular actor on a Primetime Major Network TV Show. For years, the manager and the adult actor operated on a handshake—a verbal agreement—but soon after the actor became relatively famous, he stopped paying his manager. The opposing attorney's first comment to me, stolen from Sam Goldwyn, was sarcastic: "My philosophy is that an oral contract is worth the paper it's written on." Without a written contract in hand, we litigated the case on a Breach of Oral Contract theory, investing substantial time and effort, none of which would have been necessary if a written contract had been in place. Fortunately, for my client, this case was a great example which helps prove that a verbal contract between adult talent and a Talent Manager is enforceable, especially after the adult talent ended up paying a six-figure settlement to my client, the Talent Manager.*

which often fade or change with time. People often dispute what notes or emails between one another say, and other evidence may be unclear or vague and require interpretation because some of it may have a dual or vague meaning.

Verbal agreements can also be problematic because it's much easier for the unscrupulous to deny that there was a contract or that, in better days, certain promises were made. While I am not a cynic, I am aware that people tend to remember certain conversations differently, especially when large amounts of money are at stake, or if they have other incentives not to remember certain promises that weren't reduced to writing.

So what does this mean for you, the parent? As an adult you can enter into verbal, non-written contracts with other adults, and those agreements may be enforced by a court. Thus, if you verbally promise to pay the Talent Agent a certain amount in exchange for the Talent Agent working on behalf of your child, that agreement is at least potentially enforceable.

Agreements with Talent Managers and Talent Agents are, however, far too important to leave as unwritten verbal contracts. Especially in Hollywood, the more important the agreement, the more important it is that you have a written contract. It will help you avoid problems, by maximizing the chances that you and any other service provider will understand each other clearly.

Does this mean that you should put everything anyone says to you into a formal contract? That's not practical or necessary. But even a simple email confirming what someone else told you or promised you can go a long way toward protecting your interests. If something later goes wrong or if some dispute takes place about the subject of the email, you will at least have something in writing. And some writing is often better than no writing. But most of all, the more important the promise, the more essential it is that you put it in writing with a formal written contract.

# CHAPTER 11

## CHILDREN ARE DIFFERENT

*There can be no keener revelation of a society's soul than the way in which it treats its children.*

—Nelson Mandela

## HOW CONTRACTS WITH CHILDREN DIFFER FROM CONTRACTS WITH ADULTS

Contracts with children present a unique situation. Although they appear to be just like contracts between adults and often contain similar terms and provisions, they are different. Too many of the people with whom you will interact fail to appreciate that children are different than adults in the eyes of the law. The law does not view children simply as undersized adults.

Because the law treats children differently, children require a very specialized analysis and examination. Most importantly, unlike contracts between adults, *contracts with children must be in writing to have a legally binding effect.*

It's plain and simple—regardless of how hurt or sad someone may feel, how little or much money is at stake or how fair or unfair it may seem—oral or verbal contracts between an adult and a child (other than the rare emancipated child) are never legally binding and there are no exceptions to this rule of law.

In fact, lawyers, judges, and Appellate and Supreme Court Justices use the Latin phrase, void *ab initio,* to describe such contracts, which simply means they are, by definition, void "from the beginning" or "from inception." A contract is void *ab initio* if it seriously offends law or public policy, and if different from a contract that is merely voidable at the election of one party to the contract. A verbal contract with a minor seriously offends law and public policy and is, therefore, void *ab initio.* In other words, a verbal contract with a child can be treated as if it never existed. Your child can generally just walk away from it and keep any money he or she received.

Although California law doesn't recognize the validity of oral or verbal agreements with children, many Talent Managers and Talent Agents will take your child on without a written contract because they prefer "old school" values where everyone operated on a handshake, or because they want to avoid the time and expense it takes to put together a written contract. This means, whether they realize it or not, that when it comes to their clients who are children, they're taking the risk that you and your child can, and someday just might, walk away. While it may seem appealing to keep that type of control over the situation, by simply having a loose and informal arrangement with your manager or agent, it's generally a bad idea for both parties.

If you are serious about hiring a Talent Manager or Talent Agent who will work hard for your child and be motivated to do all he or she can to advance your child's career, then it's equally smart to create the best working relationship possible. One important way to do this is by committing to the relationship and showing that commitment by entering into a binding written contract. This tells your new manager or agent that you're serious and they'll be motivated to work very hard for you—knowing that when your child is successful and a big payday materializes, they will be compensated as agreed upon and as set out in the written contract.

On the other hand, this means that the handling of the contract, which binds and obligates your child and possibly you as his parents, should be handled professionally and taken seriously. This also means that before you and your child sign a contract with a Talent Manager or Talent Agent, you, as a parent, should discuss and understand all of the terms and provision of these contracts.

So, in continuing our goal of protecting children, the remainder of this book offers a concise, detailed guide to how to understand your child's *written* contracts with Talent Managers, Talent Agents and entertainment attorneys.

# CHAPTER 12

## EVERYTHING IS NEGOTIABLE

*In business, as in life, you don't get what you deserve;*
*you get what you negotiate.*

—Dr. Chester L. Krass

Before you delve into the terms and provisions of a typical talent management, Talent Agent, or entertainment lawyer contract, be clear about one thing: every term and provision of the contract is open to negotiation.

Nothing is etched in stone.

Let me repeat—*everything* is negotiable.

Just because someone hands you a pre-printed contract that appears to be an industry standard form, and others before you have signed it, does not mean you have to take it or leave it. Remember, the person handing you the contract does not harbor the same interests as you. He may very well want to see your child succeed, but the contract is an entirely different matter. The contract provisions are there to protect their interests, not yours. If you want something else added or something changed, you will have to ask for it.

As is discussed in more detail below, the fact that every term of an agreement is negotiable doesn't mean you will or need to negotiate every term and provision. But "everything is negotiable" means what it says. This book is designed to give you the information, and with that, the confidence and strength to help you determine which issues are worth negotiating and which are not.

As tedious, difficult or annoying it might seem to understand the contracts you will be given to review, doing so must be a priority for you in order to protect your child and family. One of my goals in writing this book is to take the difficulty out of the process. I also hope that, unlike many parents, especially parents of new talent, you avoid coming from a position of desperation during the process of entering a contract with a Talent Manager, Talent Agent, entertainment lawyer, or any other representative.

Most people are overjoyed when they find that someone in the industry believes they, or their child, have sufficient talent to succeed in the glamorous and competitive world of entertainment. Let's face it; we are all a little starstruck. It is often difficult to step back and realize that you are making a very important business decision that can have huge consequences in the future. Most people are so flattered that many will sign anything that is put before them. This can be a very expensive and, in extreme situations, even a catastrophic mistake.

Admittedly, someone just breaking into the business in Hollywood is confronted with a certain amount of imbalance in almost every business deal and every other step of the way. While that may mean you need to be more flexible in what you allow and agree to, when someone offers to represent you and puts a contract in front of you for signature, it should never mean you concede or blindly agree to terms of an agreement or contract that don't feel right. Approaching the entertainment business, or any business, in this manner is a recipe for entering into bad contracts with the wrong people that can end in potentially disastrous results.

While you'll need to regularly evaluate every new relationship in light of where you or your child currently are in your careers, you shouldn't automatically accept every contract term and provision as presented. Rather, approach the whole negotiation process from a place of educated calm, hopefulness, and the belief a good deal will be made.

When you discuss the terms of your contract with the person you're considering for representation, the best thing you can do is understand what points are most important to you. These may be of secondary importance or maybe not very important at all to the person with whom you are negotiating. But when you're clear about and identify those "contract points" or "deal points," as they are sometimes called, it simplifies the process of negotiating with and interacting with Talent Managers, Talent Agents and other Hollywood insiders.

Moreover, there are two important factors that will prevent you from having to negotiate every single sentence of a contract. First, many of the paragraphs in most Hollywood contracts are fairly routine and unobjectionable. You and your child are following in the footsteps of thousands of former actors. Thus, as in any industry contract, many of the terms are there to deal with questions that come up repeatedly. The industry has settled on some approaches to dealing with these issues and a vast majority of the time those approaches work very well and can be safely followed. One such example, of many, are the SAG-AFTRA theatrical and commercial contracts for actors.

Second, and more importantly, the extent to which you can, as a practical matter, negotiate exceptions to the norm, or get some kind of individualized result, depends in large measure on how much leverage you have. There are famous stories in Hollywood about actors and singers who negotiate very specific terms into their agreements, such as the kind of candy that will be in their dressing rooms. But these kinds of terms can be negotiated only after you are sought after by name. When you have reached that status, there is only one of you, and you can ask for all sorts of things and get the other side to agree to them. But when you are just starting out, and it's perceived that many other people can replace your child in a particular role, your ability to get a producer, studio, or some other entity to take the time to negotiate very specific requests is much more limited.

Thus, while everything is negotiable, that doesn't mean that you and your child can get everything you want. This is especially true with respect to compensation. One of the most common mistakes that parents and Hollywood kids make, especially when they are relatively new, is to make demands about money that aren't in line with how well known the child is, or how many other children are perceived to be an alternative for the role that is being negotiated. Much more will be said in Part IV about money and how to negotiate the financial side of a deal, but for now, know that you are both perfectly free to ask for more money when you are presented with a contract, and that your ability to receive more money might be limited, depending on your circumstances.

This brings us back to the importance of knowing what's most important for you and your child. Because everything is negotiable, when you aren't getting something that is critical to you and your child, I encourage you to stick to your guns and, short of learning something that legitimately causes you to adjust your position, don't give in on key issues—even if you have to walk away from the deal. In the short term, while walking away may be disappointing for you and your child, if you're serious about entertainment as a career, it's best to think of the business from a long-term perspective. To do that, you should stay strong on matters of great principle that make any "walk away" decision with the advice and counsel of your Talent Agent, Talent Manager, or entertainment attorney.

# CHAPTER 13

## INFORMED CONSENT

*Any fool can know. The point is to understand.*

—Albert Einstein

A written contract wouldn't mean very much if you could later get out of it by claiming you didn't know what you were signing. The entertainment industry is particularly vigilant about making sure that doesn't happen. That is why most entertainment contracts contain a short but critical paragraph that is commonly entitled Informed Consent.

Informed Consent basically means two things. First, this provision says you acknowledge that you've read the contract, and know what you're signing. Secondly, it says that prior to signing the contract, you were given the opportunity to talk to a lawyer. This is often one of the most important provisions in an entertainment contract. If you don't read and abide by it, it could come back to haunt you.

We live in a society where people too commonly just sign forms and contracts without thoroughly reading them. It's understandable how this happens. It can be intimidating and discouraging to wade through all the legal jargon that appears in many contracts.

It is, however, imperative that you read all entertainment contracts. The potential costs and aggravation of signing a one-sided or unfavorable entertainment contract are enormous. Everyone I've ever talked with and certainly every parent who sits across from me discussing a contract dispute wishes they'd invested a little time and a few hundred dollars up front to have a lawyer look at their contract to make sure they understood what they were signing, and whether it was in their child's best interest.

Many of the contracts you are asked to sign aren't in your best interests. Why? Because contracts are usually written in favor of the person or organization that prepares them. Now, this is less likely to be true of a contract with a Talent Agent franchised with SAG-AFTRA. As you now know from Chapter 3, those Talent Agent contracts are standardized and pre-approved by both the State of California and the Guild. But the talent management contract you are asked to sign was very likely prepared by your Talent Manager's attorney. Likewise, the contract governing how much your child's deal related to his or her appearance in a movie, television series, or commercial was prepared by the lawyers for the studio or production company. So resist the temptation to sign any entertainment contract before knowing exactly what you are signing.

## SAMPLE CONTRACT LANGUAGE: INFORMED CONSENT

Here are two sample paragraphs addressing informed consent. The first indicates that you were given the chance to review the contract with a lawyer but turned it down:

> *Artist and Parent have sought and obtained or knowledgeably and willingly declined independent counsel in connection with this Agreement and the terms and provisions hereof and fully understand the terms and conditions set forth herein.*

The second is a more thorough and more common alternative. It says that you know what you are signing, were given time to review what it means, weren't forced to sign the contract, and are willingly taking the risk that you are signing the contract based on a mistaken understanding of the law:

> *Artist and Parent represent and warrant that they been advised to seek independent legal counsel regarding the terms, conditions, duties and obligations created by this Agreement and have been given an adequate opportunity to do so. Furthermore, Artist and Parent represent and warrant that they have full knowledge of any rights and obligations which they may have. Artist and Parent assume the risks of any mistake of fact or law with respect to true facts or law which are now unknown to them. Artist and Parent know and understand the contents of the Agreement and there has been no duress in the execution thereof.*

It might seem strange for an entertainment contract to bring up negative issues. Signing a contract with a Talent Agent or Talent Manager or to appear in a movie, television show, or commercial is a happy event. It's a moment that parents and their children work hard to reach. So why does the contract include all this negative talk of being forced to sign the contract, or not having time to review it?

The language in the Informed Consent paragraph isn't designed to address the time when you sign the contract. That is a happy time. It's designed to anticipate the future, when you may be less happy because some dispute or disagreement arose about what the contract means. Specifically, it's designed to limit your ability to say that the contract means something other than what the written contract shows, or that you shouldn't be held responsible for the promises you made in the contract.

For example, if you and your child's Talent Manager later disagree about whether you owe him a commission for a particular acting job, you might be tempted to argue that you didn't fully understand what the contract said about commissions, or that you honestly believed that you didn't owe the manager a commission on certain kinds of acting jobs. If this disagreement becomes the subject of a lawsuit or some other kind of formal process, the Talent Manager's attorney will show a judge, a jury, or arbitrator the Informed Consent language from the contract you signed. The Talent Manager's attorney will argue that you acknowledged you had ample opportunity to discuss the matter with counsel and knew exactly what you were agreeing to when you signed it. And many judges and juries will force you to abide by the terms of the written contract even if, in fact, you didn't read the contract, or fully understand it, or signed it without first showing it to a lawyer.

Informed Consent is one example among many that entertainment is a business. That's how Hollywood insiders view it. Every parent should, therefore, start their business relationships in the entertainment industry on an equal footing and on equal ground. When you are presented with a contract, don't sign it automatically or reflexively. This book reveals what parents of entertainment children need to know about the contracts they are most likely to be asked to sign. It also shows you when it's best to seek the advice of an experienced entertainment lawyer. Take this step seriously. It's almost always easier and cheaper to negotiate changes to a contract before you sign it than it is to change it after you have signed it. And sometimes, because of the Informed Consent language, once you sign a contract, you won't be able to change it until the contract expires.

# Summary of Part II

## What's What in Hollywood: The Unspoken Rules

- Under California law, adults can enter into verbal or oral contracts.

- Children, by contrast, cannot. An oral agreement with a child is void as a matter of law.

- The bigger the role, the more important it is that you have the agreement in writing.

- Everything in a contract is negotiable.

- How much you can change the terms of a standard written contract used in Hollywood depends on how much leverage you have.

- The more it is perceived that other talent can be substituted for your child for a particular role, the less leverage you generally have, especially with respect to compensation.

- Many provisions of standard Hollywood contracts aren't objectionable.

- The entertainment industry goes to great lengths to establish informed consent, so that people who sign contracts won't be able to get out of those contracts by later claiming they didn't understand what they were signing.

- The key to negotiating an effective contract—one that protects your child—is to know in advance what contract points are most important to you.

# PART III

*Exercising Control as a Parent*

# Part III

## Exercising Control as a Parent

Now that you know who the major players are, and some of the basic principles that guide what they do, the next step is to understand what tools you have at your disposal and how parents are asked to give others some control over their children.

This loss of control can take many forms. Sometimes parents lose control over their entertainment kids by getting locked into unfavorable contracts. The loss of control can also be more direct, as in when parents are formally asked to give up some of their legal authority.

For people who are new to the entertainment industry, many relationships involve some element of compromise and loss of control. It's not realistic or desirable to always get everything you want. Too often, however, parents of children in entertainment aren't even aware that they are at risk of losing legal control over some aspect of their child's upbringing. I designed this portion of the book to change that.

Part III includes the following chapters:

- Craig and MeShiel's Three-Year Deal
- The Contract Term (Length/Duration of the Contract)
- The Opt-Out Clause
- Power of Attorney
- Choosing the Right State Law Matters

*I think every child Star suffers through this period because
you're not the cute and charming child that you were.
You start to grow, and they want to keep you little forever.*

—Michael Jackson

In January 1999, when Craig Traylor was ten years old, his Talent
Agent, Steve Simon of the ACME Talent Agency, introduced Craig and
his mom to Talent Manager Sharyn Berg. Sharyn was the owner of her
own talent management company and already had more than fifteen
years of experience working on behalf of actors and actresses.

Sharyn expressed an interest in advising, counseling, and further
developing Craig's career by becoming his Talent Manager. MeShiel
believed that Berg was attracted to Craig as a client because he had
already achieved some early success in TV commercials, had booked a
very nice part in the motion picture *Matilda*, and also had booked a really great role opposite George Clooney on an episode of the hit NBC
television series *ER*. Craig never had a Talent Manager before, so the
idea of having Berg work with Simon, his Talent Agent, seemed like a
good one, so his mom decided to give it a try.

A few weeks after their initial meeting, Craig and MeShiel entered
into a written contract, prepared by Berg, called an "Artist's Manager's
Agreement" for personal talent management services. It was a short,
two-page contract, for a three-year term, which seemed straightforward enough to MeShiel when she signed it. Like most parents, she did
not recall actually reading it or, if she did, actually understanding all
of its details. Of course, Craig, her ten-year-old, never saw or signed
the contract. His mother wanted her young son to have a manager, so
she printed her son's name in the space designated "Artist," signed the
Agreement that was mailed to her, and returned it to Berg.

Sound familiar?

It should. Reputable Talent Agents recommend an experienced
manager, and this is how many parents and their children behave when
they sign with Talent Agents and Talent Managers. There was nothing

at all sinister or improper about the motives of either Simon or Berg. They were and are respected insiders. And the contract that MeShiel signed was typical of many that were circulating through Hollywood.

But, as you shall see, the contract that MeShiel signed that day had important and unforeseen consequences for her, her son, and Berg. Only much later did MeShiel realize that by signing the contract, she gave up control over certain aspects of the devolpoment of her son's career.

The contracts with Talent Agents and Talent Managers that you (and perhaps your child) are asked to sign are important. As explained in the following chapter, the length of the contract can help determine just how much control you can exercise as a parent.

*With kids, the days are long, but the years are short.*

—John Leguizamo, Actor

Very simply, the *term* of the contract provision deals with the length of time the contract is in effect: when it will begin and when it will end.

This is an important provision and every parent must read it carefully. Don't just gloss over it or, worse yet, give in or concede the issue of when the contract begins and when it ends without careful deliberation.

The *term* provision of the contract is typically stated as a number of years. Managers usually push for as long a term as possible because it puts them in greater control of the contract and the talent-management relationship. That said, for the Talent Manager, a longer contract could be, and often is, justified in a contract involving new talent or with an actor still in the development phase of his or her career because of the time and effort a manager may have to invest before realizing any financial return. From your child's perspective, it's usually best for the contract to be reasonably short to afford your child and your family flexibility and to keep options open. Most managers will ask for three years, while some request even longer terms. Additionally, there are ways managers can write talent management contracts, which can automatically extend the term. Automatic extensions are not always a bad idea, but watch out for them. Know what you're signing.

When looking at this section of a contract, ask yourself "If we sign this contract today, how old will my child be when the contract ends?" If your child is a six-year-old when you sign a three-year contract with an automatic three-year extension, he or she will be twelve years old when the contract ends. And a ten-year-old who enters into such a deal will be sixteen when the contract ends.

As parents, we're well aware of the differences, in everyday, ordinary things, between a six- and a twelve-year-old and a ten- and a sixteen-year-old. In many respects, children are different people at the beginning and end stages of these age ranges. When it comes to the entertainment industry, these age differences are equally significant.

Moreover, age is always significant when it comes to the availability of roles. Also, as children become teenagers and then young adults, the magnitude of these issues often grows exponentially.

In short: Carefully consider how the length of the contract relates to your child's age. Let me give you a few examples of what this section of the contract can look like in the real world. Since management contracts differ from manager to manager and place to place, let's look at four options or choices of language you might see.

Option A is a very simple sample paragraph addressing the length of the term, plain and simple, and really nothing else:

> *This Agreement commences on the date listed above and shall remain in effect for (__) years (Term or Initial Term) from the commencement date, unless the parties mutually agree otherwise in writing to terminate it earlier.*

Option B is sometimes added, so that it follows Option A. This makes the *term* provision a bit more involved, since it not only addresses the length of the term, but also "automatically" extends the initial term unless either the manager or the actor terminates the contract. If a contract has a paragraph like this, the agreement could continue indefinitely after the initial term until either of the two parties terminates it:

> *Upon expiration of the Initial Term, this Agreement shall remain in full force and effect without interruption or change unless and until any party notifies the other parties in writing by Certified Mail (Return Receipt Requested) of their intention to terminate. Such termination shall be effective immediately upon receipt.*

Option C is even more involved. The following paragraph not only gives the manager the right to an automatic extension, but the extension is for a full year (and it could be written for a greater number of years), which obviously favors the manager:

> *Artist and Parent also grant to Manager the irrevocable right and option to extend the Initial Term of this Agreement for one (1) additional period of one (1) year (Option Period). The Option Period shall be deemed to be automatically exercised by Manager unless Manager notifies Artist or Parent in writing of Manager's intention not to exercise such option not later than thirty (30) days prior to the expiration of the Initial Term.*

**ROBERT'S RECOMMENDATIONS:** I'm not a big fan of automatic renewal revisions and don't recommend them. They require a flawless calendar system and future action and planning, which even the most studious might accidentally overlook. In this particular case, the automatic extension is completely one-sided and favors the manager. It's my recommendation that any extension of the talent management agreement be a thoughtful and considered decision, not one-sided, and certainly not left to "automation" or chance.

Option D is even more complex as it not only gives the manager an automatic extension, but one based on the talent's income and one that is equal in length to the original contract term. Again, if presented with a management contract like this, carefully consider what you're signing and whether or not it's in the best interest of your child and your family:

> *If Artist's gross earnings exceed $_____ during any year of the Period, Manager will have an exclusive and irrevocable option to extend this Agreement for an additional period of time (Option Period) equal to the Initial Term and having the same terms and conditions hereof. The Option Period will commence immediately upon the expiration of the term. Said option will be exercised automatically unless Manager notifies Artist and Parent in writing of Manager's intention to terminate this Agreement not later than thirty (30) days prior to the expiration of the Initial Term.*

**ROBERT'S WARNING:** As indicated above, I am not a big fan of automatic renewal revisions and often recommend against them. Here, additionally, the automatic extension is offensively one-sided and completely favors the manager if the child is doing well. Most troubling, remember that 3+3-year contract with your ten-year-old child? Well, this provision, depending on how it is written, could lock in the *term* of the contract until your not-so-little boy or girl is eighteen or even twenty-one years old! That means your child would no longer be a child, but a young adult. That fact alone makes this a high-risk provision for any child actor or his family.

As we've seen, the term of the contract, when it will begin and end, is a very important provision and you need to read and comprehend exactly what the contract says and the impact it can have on your child's career and, potentially, family obligations and commitments.

A provision granting a Talent Manager an automatic extension is a common example of an important feature of many entertainment contracts that could potentially impact other provisions. The contract term might, for example, last three years, but some of the obligations under the contract might last longer than that. Many parents, agents, and managers miss this point. Just as a lawyer's duty to keep his client's information confidential continues after the lawyer has stopped working for the client, certain obligations imposed on Talent Managers, Talent Agents, and parents may also last beyond the date on which the contract ends. Many of these obligations relate to money and how it is paid. Part IV will discuss these financial obligations in greater detail. But the general idea is this: If you want to fully protect yourself and your family, you have to keep an eye out for any obligations that the contract imposes, even after the contract has officially ended.

# CHAPTER 16

## THE OPT-OUT CLAUSE

*Nature provides exceptions to every rule.*

—Margaret Fuller
Journalist, Women's Rights Advocate

An underappreciated provision in your contract gives you and your child the right, under certain circumstances, to get out of the contract. If this language is included in the contract, it gives you more control and helps make sure the *term* provision isn't totally one–sided. As a young lawyer, one of my mentors taught me to look carefully for "not only what *is in the contract* but also what *isn't in the contract*." I pass this wisdom on to you, so you'll look for the absence of a provision commonly called an Opt-Out Clause or an Exit Clause.

This clause, in one form or another, is already built in to talent agency contracts. For your protection, I'd also like to see this clause added to your contract with Talent Managers. Specifically, it gives your child, under certain limited and reasonable circumstances, a way out of the contract before its end date. This provision describes under what conditions an actor may terminate the agreement as a way of providing balance to the contract. Given the fact that the relationship between an actor and a Talent *Manager* is unlike that of an actor with a Talent *Agent*, the same strict exit clause, when seen in Talent Agent agreements, is probably unreasonable. When it comes to the opt-out clause, you should take into account that managers need more time to work and develop a child's career.

Unfortunately, an opt-out clause in a contract that a manager presents for signature is rare and this is simply unfair to the actor and his family. I suggest including language in the contract that allows you to opt out if the manager doesn't generate results for you within a reasonable amount of time. Something as simple as the following language can make all the difference to you and yet, still remain fair to your Talent Manager:

*If manager fails to assist in the progression of Artist's career and in conjunction with a licensed Talent Agent fails to obtain a bona*

*fide offer of employment from a responsible employer during a pe-
riod in excess of six (6) consecutive months during the term hereof,
provided Artist is ready, able, and willing to accept employment,
either party hereto shall have the right to terminate this contract
by a notice in writing to such effect sent to the other party by registered or certified mail to the last known address of such party.*

In summary, it's usually best for the contract between a child and his
manager to be reasonably short in duration, so that the minor and his
or her family can keep their options open if the manager isn't performing reasonably. If, however, you and your family conclude that you've
found a great manager, and he refuses to have a reasonably short-term
agreement, be sure to protect your child and family by including a reasonable opt-out or exit clause. This clause will provide some protection
for you and your child if things between you and your Talent Manager
ultimately don't work out as originally hoped for or initially expected.

# CHAPTER 17

## POWER OF ATTORNEY

*Our children are not for sale at any price.*

—Beverly to Radue
*Star Trek: The Next Generation*

Be very careful in giving any Talent Manager, Talent Agent, or any other representative the power of attorney to act or do things, legally, on behalf of your child. When you give this power to someone, it means you gave that person the power to act legally on behalf of your child, with or without your knowledge, and with or without further permission or ongoing authority. This privilege can include things such as cashing checks without your ever seeing them, signing contracts without your knowledge or your input, and a host of other privileges.

Giving this power away can be the equivalent, depending on how the provision reads, to giving away the absolute power over every facet of your child's professional career, including all contractual and financial decisions. Giving up this power opens the door for decisions, both bad and good, influencing your child and potentially your family. It can be devastating if you inadvertently sign with an unethical manager, as giving up this power exposes your child, and potentially your family, to misuse and the risk for financial ruin.

The bottom line: you should give very limited or preferably no power of attorney to a Talent Agent or Talent Manager, or other representative—especially when you haven't worked with them before.

A sample power of attorney paragraph, which I recommend *against*, might read something like this:

*Artist and Parent appoint Manager as Artist's lawful Attorney-in-Fact, to perform any and all services, execute any and all documents, and do any and all things necessary pursuant to this Agreement. To reinforce this authority, Parent agrees, upon request, to execute before a Notary Public a separate Power of Attorney for Manager. The authority granted by this section is coupled with an interest and shall be irrevocable during the term of this Agreement. Nothing in this section shall be construed to allow Artist or Parent to revoke Manager's right, if any, to receive payments or endorsed checks on behalf of Artist, as provided in this as provided in this Agreement until sixty (60) days after expiration of this Agreement.*

Although limited Power of Attorney provisions may be appropriate, they often raise a practical problem. For example, if a Talent Manager were to show someone a power-of-attorney clause that was drafted to be limited, that other person might be inexperienced with the law or otherwise mistakenly conclude that the manager had unbridled power. In short, if you sign even a limited Power of Attorney, how will you know to what extent it is being used, and what would prevent those unschooled in the law from relying upon it? This is a problem that has led to misunderstandings and disputes, or in a worst-case scenario, to expensive litigation.

Finally, there is an additional important misconception related to the Power of Attorney. As a parent, you don't actually have the right to give a Power of Attorney away to a Talent Agent or Talent Manager or anyone else on behalf of your child. A parent can obligate himself, but from a strict legal perspective, a parent cannot sign a Power of Attorney and authorize someone to act on your child's behalf. As discussed in Part V, additional steps are required to obligate children who enter into entertainment contracts. Again, while a Power of Attorney by itself is not sufficient to do that, those uninformed in the law may honor a Power of Attorney that appears legally effective.

# CHAPTER 18

## THE IMPORTANCE OF CHOOSING THE RIGHT STATE LAW

*It's the little details that are vital. Little things
make big things happen.*

—John Wooden

The last page or two of many contracts in Hollywood contain a short paragraph that is easy to overlook, but which really matters. This provision, typically called Choice of Law, could end up being the single most helpful or harmful provision in the entire contract. Which state's laws apply to a contract can completely change how one interprets a contract.

This is particularly important if there is ever a lawsuit or other dispute about the contract. I've taken on new clients who were forced into extensive and expensive litigation on this issue alone, because they did not read or understand the provision before they signed the contract. Let's make sure you know what Choice of Law provisions are all about and why they are important.

It is important to select the correct state law to interpret a contract because some states have much more sophisticated entertainment-related laws than others. California has been at the heart of the entertainment industry for more than a century. That's where Motion Pictures and television shows were first made. Therefore, you probably won't be surprised to learn that most of the early *landmark* cases and the majority of the laws related to the entertainment industry originated in California.

Indeed, even today, California, followed closely only by New York, has the largest body of laws pertaining to the entertainment industry. Moreover, California law has the longest history of establishing laws and regulations that are specifically intended to protect children in entertainment. One of the early triggers for this was a shocking scandal in the 1930s involving child Star Jackie Coogan, "the youngest self-made millionaire in history." He later discovered that his mother and stepfather squandered his childhood fortune. The uproar from the scandal led to the passage of new California laws, the first of their kind in the United States. *The Coogan Laws* were written to protect the money that child actors earn. This is just one example of how California has long regulated the industry, with laws on an array of subjects discussed throughout this book.

California law continues to be assertive about protecting children in entertainment. This doesn't happen by accident. There are well organized activists in the state who devote themselves to advocating on behalf of children in entertainment, including Paul Petersen, founder of *A Minor Consideration*, Toni Casala, founder of *ChildrenInFilm. com*, and Anne Henry and Paula Dorn, co-founders of the *BizParentz Foundation*. Other remarkable groups and people, such as the members of the Screen Actors Guild's *Young Performers Committee*, bring attention to a range of issues, virtually guaranteeing that California will remain sensitive about protecting children in entertainment.

Of course, New York, with its notable contributions to the entertainment industry, has also developed laws related to entertainment and the protection of children in the industry, including the very recent regulations related exclusively to child performers that took effect April 1, 2013, under the New York Code of Rules and Regulations (NYCRR). Still, no state has entertainment industry protections in place quite like those in California. Certainly all states have a compelling interest in protecting their citizens and children, and this compels most states to turn first to California, and then often to New York, for guidance on how to handle entertainment contracts and disputes.

As a result of how and where Entertainment Law developed, where most production companies maintain their principal offices, and where talent agencies and managers work, the majority of entertainment contracts will include a provision that says that the laws of the State of California or the State of New York apply. However, be very cautious if the contract designates the law of some other state as the applicable choice of law for your contract. In fact, some states, especially those who still have a strong agrarian economy and at one time relied upon children to help during the harvest, have very scant laws, if any, protecting minors in the workplace.

In my experience, you'll likely want the laws of the State of California to apply regardless of any other factor, whenever possible. California has the clearest and best laws in place, which specifically affect the entertainment industry and protect your child. Additionally, probably more than any other state, there are numerous judges, arbitrators, mediators, and lawyers in California who fully understand the inner workings of the entertainment business. Therefore, the decision-makers in California are more likely to be knowledgeable when it comes to entertainment-industry-related disputes.

Here's an example of what you will normally want to see regarding Choice of Law in your talent agreement:

*California procedural and substantive law shall apply to any disputes arising from, or relating to, this Agreement without regard to any other choice of law rules. Further, the appropriate venue for enforcement of this Agreement is in Los Angeles County, California. Each party submits to a personal jurisdiction before that court. This provision is valid and enforceable irrespective of the place of execution of this Agreement or the performance of this Agreement.*

## CASE STUDY

*A few years ago, a child was on a reality television series with other children. The production took place outside of both California and New York. The labor laws of the state where the production took place were scant, at best, when it came to protecting children in entertainment. After the child was seriously injured during the production, I was asked to represent the child and the child's family. Because the contract was unclear as to the Choice of Law, the very first issue that had to be decided was which law applied—the law of the state where the production company had its principal offices, the law where the contract was signed, the law where the minor resided, or the law of the state where the minor was injured. I argued heavily and vigorously on behalf of my client that California law (which was clearly most favorable) should be applied in the lawsuit. The defense disputed this with equal vigor. Enormous resources were expended by all parties while resolving this key dispute before we could even reach the substantive evaluation of the case itself. Everyone knew that the judge's decision would have a huge impact on our success (or failure) moving forward. Fortunately, we prevailed in our argument that California law applied and the case was thereafter quickly resolved to the satisfaction of all involved.*

If a contract provides that the laws of some state other than California apply, be careful. As indicated above, the laws of other states may be unfavorable to your entertainment kids in some way. Moreover, it can be unnecessarily expensive to be involved in a lawsuit in which you are in one state and a different state's laws control how the contract is interpreted. This is because most lawyers are only authorized to represent you in the state in which the lawyer has his or her other practice. That means that you may have to hire two lawyers, one in your state, and one in the state that is named in the contract's Choice of Law provision. If you live and work in California, you can avoid this expense and protect your child more effectively by making sure your contract is controlled by California law (or, in some limited circumstances, the law of New York State).

In short, Choice of Law issues are important. Pay attention to the language of the contract that describes it. It's too important to ignore.

# Summary of Part III

## Exercising Control As A Parent

If you want to protect your child in Hollywood, you need to be able to identify specific ways in which you may be giving up too much control as a parent. In Part III, we learned that you can give up too much control by:

- Entering into a contract that is too long, given the age of your son or daughter.

- Failing to identify that the contract has an automatic renewal clause.

- Forgetting to include a reasonable opt-out clause in a contract with a Talent Manager or other representative.

- Agreeing to give a Talent Manager or Talent Agent a Power of Attorney, especially if you have not worked with him or her before.

- Signing an agreement with a Talent Manager or Talent Agent that applies the law of a state other than California (or, in some limited cases, New York).

If you avoid the mistakes listed above, you will be miles ahead of many other parents of Hollywood's entertainment children. Specifically, you will put yourself in a situation where, as a parent, the contract you signed won't undermine your ability to act in the best interests of your child.

There are, of course, many reasons why parents and their children are interested in the world of entertainment. Money certainly isn't the only or primary reason to pursue a dream in Hollywood. You will, however, be able to protect your child more effectively on his/her road to fame if you understand the basics of how actors and actresses earn money and get paid in Hollywood. That's the subject matter of Part IV.

# PART IV

*Follow the Money:*
*Understanding Compensation*

# PART IV

## FOLLOW THE MONEY: UNDERSTANDING COMPENSATION

Fame and Fortune.

There's no denying that people are attracted to the entertainment industry in part because of a desire to make a lot of money and a perception that Hollywood provides an avenue to do that. As a parent of an entertainment child, it is understandable to want your child to become financially successful in the industry—it is one of the lures and perks of the business.

There is, unfortunately, a great deal of misinformation and hype about money in Hollywood. Huge TV and movie stars and international icons understandably get most of the attention. It's hard not to be swayed by news that a movie star earns $20 million for the lead role in a Motion Picture or that the star of a hit television show earns six figures for each weekly episode. However, the more relevant questions for parents and entertainment kids are: (1) Why do stars earn as much as they do? and (2) What can you reasonably expect as your child's entertainment career progresses?

Hollywood is fundamentally a business. As a parent, you can't protect yourself or act in the best interests of your child unless you have at least a basic understanding of how people in entertainment earn money and how they get paid. Likewise, you won't be able to evaluate offers that are made to your child, whether directly or through your Talent Agent or entertainment attorney, unless you know what's typical in terms of compensation.

Part IV will teach you what you need to know so that you, too, can understand and "follow the money." Part IV includes the following chapters:

- Craig and MeShiel Pay a 15% Commission
- Talent Agent's and Talent Manager's Commissions
- Key Deal points in Televesion, Film, and Commercial Contracts
- Your Hollywood Labor Unions
- What Do Actors Earn in Film, TV, and Commercials
- Health Insurance and Other Benefits
- Cost and Expenses
- Who Gets Paid First?
- Understanding Audit Rights

# CHAPTER 19

## CRAIG AND MESHIEL PAY A 15%
## TALENT MANAGEMENT COMMISSION

*What we seek is some kind of compensation
for what we put up with.*

—Haruki Murakami, Author

The talent management contract that MeShiel signed in January, 1999, contained a commission clause that provided that Talent Manager Sharyn Berg was to receive 15% of the "gross monies" Craig earned throughout the three-year term of the contract. The 15% figure caught MeShiel's eye as she was reviewing the contract. It was the one aspect of the contract she remembered most vividly. MeShiel signed the contract because she had heard that this was a typical commission. And it was.

The contract contained additional commission language that MeShiel didn't remember quite as clearly. Under the contract, Berg would also be entitled to receive a 15% commission on money Craig earned *after the agreement ended* if the money was earned as a result of employment Craig had secured when Berg was his manager. This is a great cautionary example of an obligation in the contract that might exist even after the contract has been terminated.

This is a common provision in talent management contracts. Sharyn Berg was perfectly within her rights to request a commission for work that she helped secure. And MeShiel did exactly what almost all parents do when presented with this kind of language; she signed the contract without further thought.

As it turned out, the contract language relating to Craig's future earnings was a big deal. To understand why, we need to review how Hollywood generally treats commissions.

# CHAPTER 20

## TALENT AGENT'S AND TALENT MANAGER'S COMMISSIONS

*If you're good at something, never do it for free.*

—The Joker, *The Dark Knight Rises*

Traditionally, Talent Agents charge a 10% commission for monies earned in a SAG-AFTRA Union Film, television series or commercial, and 20% for print and non-union projects. Talent Managers, by contrast, will charge 15% for all work booked, whether union or non-union. Some Talent Managers charge 10% and a small number charge 20%, but that higher rate is really something we saw in years gone by— not so much in today's economic climate. Thus, the 15% commission MeShiel and Craig paid Talent Manager Sharyn Berg was typical.

The real question, however, is 10% or 15% percent of what?

Commissions are commonly calculated against gross earnings. In other words, the commission is calculated against everything the talent earns—everything! It's charged against all income earned—before taxes and before Coogan account deductions. Again, whether it's a TV show, feature film, short film, commercial, print project, role earned in live theater, voice-over spot, speech, public appearance, or anything else booked in the entertainment industry. For each of the revenue sources identified above, "gross earnings" also includes corresponding future streams of revenue, such as residual income and merchandising royalties.

Unless you specifically exclude something while negotiating a contract, and that exclusion is written into the contract, compensation against gross revenues means against *everything* your child earns. This even includes projects the Talent Agent or Talent Manager has nothing to do with, such as one booked directly by the actor or his parent. Furthermore, if a child receives payment in the form of a trip to Walt Disney World or a new bicycle, 15% of the value of those items would technically and normally be included in the calculation.

While many Talent Agents and Talent Managers might let smaller items slide, they are not likely to be as forgiving, nor should they be, with more significant non-cash payments. The only qualifier to the word "everything" is if the contract specifically states something is excluded.

## COMMISSIONABLE INCOME FOR TALENT AGENTS

Although the concept of gross revenue is broadly defined, a variety of factors determines whether commissions are owed for certain revenue-generating activities. Thus, when it comes to paying a commission to a Talent Agent, it's very important to understand exactly what is commissionable and what is non-commissionable. The answer to that question depends on a variety of circumstances, including where you live and what type of project you booked. As odd as it may seem, commission obligations differ in Los Angeles, Chicago, Detroit, Atlanta, Washington D.C. and Hawaii on the one hand, and New York and all other cities on the other. The SAG-AFTRA website has a chart detailing all of your commission obligations and describes when no commissions are payable, no matter where you live. Here are a few of the highlights:

For television and theatrical projects, if the location of your "original employment" is Los Angeles, no commission is payable if your income is at SAG scale. For commission on such projects to be payable in Los Angeles, employment must be at least ten percent above SAG scale. On the other hand, in New York, commission is payable even if the income is only at SAG scale. For commercials, commission is payable on SAG scale employment, regardless of where you might live or whether the income includes that extra 10%. When it comes to commission on "residuals," the commission obligations differ greatly depending on a number of factors, and although those details are beyond the scope of this book, they are certainly worth reviewing on the SAG-AFTRA website, provided below.

In addition, you owe no commissions to Talent Agents in the following categories of compensation, no matter where you live: travel expenses, paid living expenses, per diems, mileage, wardrobe allowances, special hair, dress, prop allowances, penalty payments where you are paid a late payment or for a meal period violation, a forced call, or for rest-period violations.

For more detailed information go to: *http://www.sagaftra.org/what-commissionable*, and be sure to click the link titled "News & Advisories: Fine Print," which provides a detailed chart of commissionable obligations and non-commissionable obligations to Talent Agents.

## Commissions in Talent Manager Contracts

Here are two sample provisions addressing the subject of commissionable obligations in a talent management contract. The first is a short, simple, and understandable paragraph. The second, a series of paragraphs, is more elaborate and more common.

The first version basically states exactly what is mentioned above—that the manager earns his percentage on all gross income except for money the child gets as a *per diem*, or for travel and wardrobe, as these items are not considered "income":

> *As compensation for Manager's services under this Agreement, Artist and Parent shall pay Manager a commission of _____ percent (__%) of all gross monies or other considerations paid to Artist and/or Parent, whether directly or indirectly, for Artist's services, including use of Artist's voice, likeness or image, including payments for merchandising or any other promotional efforts, or bona fide offers of employment made during the term of this Agreement that are ultimately accepted (even if after the termination or expiration of this Agreement) in a form substantially similar to the bona fide offer ("Gross Earnings"), regardless of when Artist or Parent may receive such payments. Gross Earnings shall not include any per diem payments or reimbursements for travel or wardrobe, or employment remuneration or other receipts unrelated to the entertainment industry.*

The longer version includes a more intimidating series of paragraphs, basically saying that the manager is entitled to commission on contracts entered (booked) and/or even those substantially negotiated during the term, plus post-termination increases, extensions, amendments, renewals, substitutions and resumptions. Four or five paragraphs in the contract may be devoted to discussing the commission. Let's take this paragraph by paragraph and make some sense of it.

The first paragraph, essentially identical to the paragraph discussed above, says:

> *As compensation for Manager's services under this Agreement, Artist and Parent agree to pay, and Artist and Parent hereby assign to Manager, irrevocably, as and when received by or on behalf of Artist during the Term, a sum equal to ___ percent (__%) of any and all gross revenues and other consideration of any kind or*

*nature whatsoever ("Gross Earnings") which Artist and/or Parent may receive as a result of Artist's activities in the entertainment industry, exclusive of any per diem payments or reimbursements for travel or wardrobe, as follows:*

Then the second paragraph explains in detail all the areas of the entertainment industry covered by the contract. This is a grocery list of items (everything from Film and television to endorsements). As a parent you must scour the list so you understand everything covered and everything on which you may have to pay commission, so that you can intelligently converse with the manager if you wish to exclude one or more of the items on the list. In addition, this paragraph says you will pay the commission *throughout the world in perpetuity, and without limitation*, a legal phrase that means *everything earned and continuing forever*, including not just earnings in the USA, but earnings throughout the world. Look at how it reads:

*Without limiting the foregoing, commissionable activities shall include all activities in connection with music and singing-related engagements of all types and kinds, live or on-camera theatrical engagements, feature Film and television production, hosting, commercials, radio, records, publishing, magazines, newspapers, books, concerts, shows, voiceovers, print, Internet (including websites and webcasts), all forms of social media and technology, cellular phones, product endorsements, product placement, personal appearances, and the use of Artist's name, voice, likeness and talents in connections therewith and for purposes of merchandising, advertising, product endorsements, product placement and/ or trade domestically or internationally, throughout the world in perpetuity and without limitation.*

I've seen and represented many people in lawsuits involving disputes over commissions. Invariably, the above provision is at the heart of the dispute. Every parent must exercise great care before agreeing to this provision. Parents must understand that signing this contract may very well require paying commissions and fees to the manager that were not anticipated or expected at the time the contract was signed. The most problematic language is that which suggests that the child (and maybe even the parent) agrees to pay commissions on payment "increases" and "extensions" of the original contract, etc. This provision frequently causes the most conflict, grounds for misunderstanding, and dissatisfaction.

This third paragraph explains exactly what the phrase "Gross Earnings" means—again, it means all income, no exceptions:

> The term "Gross Earnings" shall include, without limitation, salaries, earnings, fees, royalties, bonuses, damages and other awards pursuant to claims, suits and other proceedings, partnership and joint venture interests and Motion Pictures or other entertainment package fees earned or received directly or indirectly by Artist or Artist's Parent, heirs, executors, administrators or assigns or by any other person, firm or corporation on Artist's behalf.

**CASE STUDY**

*I serve as legal counsel for a well-known star for whom I was easily able to negotiate a clause in his talent management contract that excluded commissions from all book and autograph signings and public appearances. These activities were already being handled by the actor's publicist. As a result, the actor avoided the additional commission on the specifically excluded work, and this was fair to everyone since the manager would not, in reality, contribute to this process or the bookings.*

This fourth paragraph is equally important. It says that, even if a given project is not booked by the time the contract ends, but was "substantially negotiated during the term of the contract," presumably by the agent or attorney, the child owes commissions on each of those projects as well. Thus, for example, the following language could generate a commission for the Talent Manager if the Talent Agent substantially negotiated a deal in July, but another person finished negotiating in September:

> Artist and Parent agree to pay Manager a commission at the rate provided above following the expiration of the Term with respect to all Gross Earnings pursuant to any engagements, contracts and agreements entered into or "Substantially Negotiated" during the Term including all increases, extensions, amendments, renewals, substitutions or resumptions thereof. The term "Substantially Negotiated" means any contract for the services of Artist where a confirming letter or deal memorandum has been sent by either party to the contract or where Artist's Talent Agent fairly believes that a contractual commitment will be forthcoming.

## LOAN-OUT COMPANIES

Once your child starts to earn substantial income, their tax professionals often advise them to set up companies, called loan-out companies,
through which they perform their acting services. In doing so, income
is legally directed to his loan-out company rather than directly to the
performer. This last paragraph relating to commissions says that if the
money for a project is paid to a company owned by the actor, instead
of directly to the actor under his or her name, commission is still owed,
of course, to the Talent Agent or Talent Manager. This provision is fair
and reasonable; it protects the Talent Manager by preventing the talent
from avoiding the responsibility to pay commission simply by setting
up an intermediary company to handle the money made by the actor, singer or other talent. If you see this type of language, do not be
alarmed or concerned. Here's a typical way this concept is phrased in
a manager's contract:

> *The terms "Artist" and "Parent" include any corporation or limited
> liability company (LLC) owned, partly or wholly, or controlled, di-
> rectly or indirectly, by the Artist and/or Parent or the Artist's and/
> or Parent's family.*

Every parent should exercise great care to ensure that he understands
fully the commission language in the contract. The four or five paragraphs identified above are representative, but there are numerous
variations. Certain language is particularly problematic. Specifically, if
any contract demands compensation for the long term, *in perpetuity*,
it should raise a red flag in the mind of any parent. If anyone presents
you or your child with a contract that includes language about commissions that is as extensive as the one described above, seek the advice
of an experienced entertainment lawyer.

# CHAPTER 21

## KEY DEAL POINTS IN TELEVISION, FILM, AND COMMERCIAL CONTRACTS

*A negotiator should observe everything.*
*You must be part Sherlock Holmes, part Sigmund Freud.*

—Victor Kiam, entrepreneur and owner
of the New England Patriots ('88–'91)

## WHAT ARE THE "KEY DEAL POINTS" IN AN ACTOR'S CONTRACT?

*Key Deal Points* are the terms that all of the parties have to agree upon before they can negotiate the finer points of the talent contract.

As discussed throughout this book, entertainment contracts with Talent Managers and Talent Agents contain many deal points. This chapter redirects our focus to address key deal points related to television, independent Film, Major Motion Picture, and commercial contracts, and those that are particularly important to children in entertainment.

Many entertainment lawyers generally prioritize deal points in two or more categories, such as "Main Deal Points" and "Secondary Deal Points" or "Minor Deal Points." I have not done so in this chapter for the simple reason that without personally speaking with you I cannot tell you what is most important to your child and your family and what might be less important. Instead, I encourage you to consider all of the deal points in this chapter and prioritize those that are "key" according to your personal preferences and on the advice of counsel.

In the entertainment industry, key deal points are often reduced to a short-form contract called a Deal Memo that outlines just those points and includes a provision that a more complete, long-form agreement will be drafted at a future date. Deal Memos are typically created so the parties can start working together immediately until the long-form agreement is finalized.

Many entertainment attorneys, including myself, resist the use of

Deal Memos over concerns that the finer details of the contract have not been negotiated or considered, and that this lack of attention to detail can open up potential problems down the road. Our concern is that the long-form agreements never get around to being finalized. Despite this, we tend to see the use of deal memos regularly in the entertainment business. Either way, a deal memo can be construed as a legally binding contract, and should you sign one you must assume that it can be upheld as binding on the parties.

Before getting into the specific deal points, let's conceptually discuss the *areas* or *topics* that are fundamental to these types of contracts. This list is not intended to cause concern or intimidate you, but rather simply to make you think.

- Other than your child, who are the *parties* to the contract?
- What is your child *getting* by entering into the contract?
- What is your child *giving*, and what might you be giving in exchange for what you are getting by entering into the contract?
- What *obligations does your child have*, and what obligations might you have, by entering into the contract?
- What *rights does your child have*, and what rights might you have, by entering into the contract?
- What *agreements and promises are your child making*, and what agreements and promises might you be making, by entering into the contract?
- What *agreements and promises are the other parties making* by entering into the contract?
- What *protections* are in place for you and your child?
- What happens *if there is a dispute* between your child and the other parties—how are disputes handled?
- What *laws govern* the contract?

The above topics are intended to impress upon you that many of the provisions in a contract are interrelated and overlap, one impacting the other.

Now, as we turn to the discussion of specific deal points, keep in mind that I wrote the remainder of this chapter to help educate you and your family about some of the many deal points that you should consider. My goal is to make you be more confident and educated when it comes to discussing deal points as your Talent Agent or entertainment attorney closes deals for your child. However, first a word of caution: While one of the reasons I am writing this book is because I want educated and confident parents, I am not trying to create brassy and over-confident parents who push their Talent Agents and entertainment attorneys so hard that they lose out on great opportunities for their children. Nor am I trying to create parents who conclude that they know more about negotiating and closing a nice deal for their child than their Talent Agent or entertainment attorney. With that word of advice, let's discuss specific deal points.

To begin, remember that what may be an important deal point to one person may not mean very much to someone else. This is because the importance of a particular deal point can depend on outside factors, including where someone is along their career path, or if someone has a unique or special need or requirement. For example, a seven-foot center for the Los Angeles Lakers who is making a cameo appearance in a Motion Picture might "need" a larger on-set trailer or dressing room, and while your seven-year-old daughter might think it would be really neat to have one, it may not be a priority deal point. Likewise, while an actor with "special needs" might have certain requirements that should be negotiated into a contract, those same requirements may not even be a part of the discussion for someone else.

## Fourteen Deal Points That Apply to Contracts for Children or Adults

### Compensation

*Base Compensation*, also commonly referred to as Fixed Compensation, is essentially the guaranteed money that your child will make regardless of whether the independent movie, Major Motion Picture, television drama or comedy, or television commercial is actually ever shown in the theaters, on a television set or on a computer. Since this is the only money your child can count on earning, this is almost always a very important deal point.

*Built-in Compensation Increases,* frequently called "bumps." Be sure to seek this on all Series Regular roles for television. These built-in compensation increases, often 4–5% per "series year," are first calculated against the base compensation of "series year one" and thereafter based on the increased compensation in each subsequent year, so over time this built-in "raise" can be significant.

*Contingent Compensation* can also be a point of negotiation, in addition to base compensation. As the term implies, contingent compensation is only paid if something in addition to working on the project takes place. Contingent compensation is a rather broad term and to understand it one must discuss the various types of contingent compensation that exist, which include residual income, use fees, profit participation, deferred compensation, and bonuses. Let's discuss each.

*Use Fees/Residual Income* is the money paid to a performer when, for example, a television show or commercial plays over and over again, or a Motion Picture is broadcast repeatedly on television. SAG-AFTRA union contracts have elaborate schedules describing exactly how these income payments are made, and this subject is further discussed in Chapter 23. However, parents should be aware that on virtually all non-union productions, whether television, Motion Picture or commercials, your child will be asked to sign a contract with a provision that waives all rights to receiving use fees or residual income.

*Profit Participation* income is the money that an actor or actress can potentially receive as a percentage of the "net profits" of a feature Film, and can also include the profits earned from merchandising sales from those Films. As for television, a series regular contract can often be negotiated to include profit participation of a percentage of net profit merchandising income related to the use of the actor's "in character" name or likeness. The term "profit participation" is used synonymously or interchangeably with the terms "back end points" or "points on the back end" and simply means a percentage of the net profits.

However, it is the definition of the term "net profits" that will determine whether your child's profit participation clause is virtually worthless or will potentially generate significant revenue streams. While the definition has been the subject of numerous articles, treatises, and even court opinions, most would agree that in its most basic form the term refers to money which remains after the costs of making, marketing, advertising, financing, and distributing a Motion Picture have been repaid to the producer from its gross profits. In short, net profits refer to the monies left over after most everything else has been deducted, and whatever percentage you have negotiated will be calculated against that lesser figure. And that definition is likely the most favorable scenario. The best tip one can offer is that you should never be too impressed with a producer or studio offering a percentage of net profits on a project, unless they are willing to alter the definition and method used to calculate the net profit figure upon which your percentage is based. If you can negotiate some form of gross profit participation deal, then you may have something of real value.

*Deferred Compensation* is typically a deal point seen in an independent Motion Picture, and generally refers to a promised or guaranteed sum of money that is only paid if and when a Film production company recoups all of its costs in making a Film. This payment provision is often used if the producer's Film budget is insufficient to pay the actor all of the upfront base compensation that the actor has negotiated.

*Bonus Compensation* is income paid to an actor or actress if a particular goal is achieved, such as crossing a particular box-office-receipts milestone or reaching a specified earnings target.

## Credits

*Screen Credit* is what comes first to mind for most. How screen credits are determined is a key deal point in every television and Film contract. This provision, if properly drafted, would include such things as the location of an actor's screen credits—whether, for example, in the main titles or end titles, and how an actor's name appears, whether alone on a single screenshot ("single card") or on a screenshot shared with other actors ("shared card"). In some cases this clause might detail things such as the font size and style as compared to how credits are given to other actors, although these latter issues are traditionally left to the producers' discretion.

*Paid Ads Credit* is an additional provision that, if negotiated, details whether specific name credit must also appear in all paid advertisements, posters, and other promotional materials, whether in print or digital format, including the Internet.

## Term

As was discussed in Chapter 15, the term of the contract defines when the contract begins and when the contract ends. Simply stated, it is the period of time in which the contract is in effect, although provisions of the contract can impose certain performance requirements or payments even beyond the term of the contract.

As is explained in more detail below, the term of a contract for a movie actor has different deal points than, for example, a television contract.

In terms of a Motion Picture contract, an important deal point for almost everyone is the start date of the project, and more so, your child's particular start date—which might be different from the first on-set production date. Likewise, the number of shoot days required of your child is a key deal point. While a Major Motion Picture might have a fifty-day shoot schedule, rarely is any particular actor or actress obligated to be on set all fifty days. In fact, smaller roles might require a day or two, a week or two, or just a portion of the entire shoot schedule. Tying these details down is an important deal point.

In terms of television, for Series Regular roles, the issue of length of service and/or the term relates to both the number of years of the contract and also the number of guaranteed episodes your child can negotiate per season. As discussed further below, it's common to be asked (if not required) to sign a six-series-year option for a Fall Season start (equivalent to 22–23 episodes), or a six- and-one-half-series-year option for a mid-season start contract. People often ask why networks request (or even require) a six-year or, even more often, a six-and-one-half-year contract. It seems like such an odd and random request, but it isn't. Networks try to maximize what is commonly called the seven-year-rule. Under California law, a contract for personal services may not be enforced beyond seven years from the commencement of the date when the services began. This historic rule dates back to the 1940s, when it was the subject of a famous precedent-setting case against Warner Bros. It can now be found as law in Section 2855(a) of the California Labor Code. Because studios can't force someone to sign a personal services contract that is longer than seven years, they do the next best thing—require a six- or six-and-one-half-year contract.

Included in the key deal points for a television contract is the number of episodes per series year. The contract will indicate the number of episodes per cycle and the minimum guaranteed number of episodes in which a particular performer will appear. Some actors negotiate six guaranteed episodes of thirteen, others secure ten of thirteen, and the main stars of the show are usually offered thirteen of thirteen, the latter of which is commonly called "All Shows Produced." Obviously, the greater the guaranteed number of shows you negotiate, the greater the guaranteed compensation. On television, compensation for Series Regulars is generally paid on a per-episode basis. A higher number of guaranteed episodes therefore means more money and exposure.

### Favored Nations

*Favored Nations* provisions are often overlooked. A "favored nations" clause, which can be very valuable, states that no other actor can receive a better deal or a more advantageous position than the person with the "favored nations" clause in his or her contract. The "favored nations" clause is typically tied to particular deal points, such as compensation deal points and/or credit deal points. Occasionally, a "favored nations" clause can be tied to the entire contract, but this is less common. "Favored nations" clauses sometimes have limitations, such as a phrase stating that an actor is granted "favored nations" privileges only to other actors in a "similar position" on the Film. That means that if your child was a "supporting actor" in a feature Film, his/her "favored nations" rights would be limited to matching those of other supporting actors in the Film, but not necessarily the stars. Still, negotiating a "favored nations" provision can be a very valuable asset in your child's contract.

### Pay or Play

*Pay or Play* clauses are potentially a most powerful deal point up for negotiation in your child's contract. The "pay or play" clause requires the television or Motion Picture production company to pay the actor the negotiated base compensation (or some other negotiated amount) regardless of whether the actor, your child, performs services and whether or not his or her services are used in the production. In short, a "pay or play" provision essentially guarantees payment of the compensation provisions of the contract—almost regardless of what happens.

### Studio Guarantee on the Contract

*Guarantee to Compensation*—or better yet a guarantee from the Studio related to the entire contract—is one of the most important and possibly the most overlooked deal points in a talent contract. Having such a provision protects against the situation where, for example, a Limited Liability Company (LLC) is created for the sole purpose of conducting all business related to, let's say, a feature Film project (commonly called a "one-off" LLC) and the LLC goes bust. Without the "Guarantee" on the contract from the Studio, the actor may never get paid, or if the actor was paid for his or her performance for working on the Film, the actor may never get paid on the merchandising, back-end points, or receive other ancillary income created after the actual shoot schedule.

### Series Relocation Fees
It makes sense to negotiate, up front, for series relocation fees in the event that the producer or studio elects to move the shoot location of, for example, a television series. Although relocation is relatively rare, this happened in 2008 on the ABC hit television show *Ugly Betty* which, after two successful seasons, moved from Los Angeles to New York City in order to, reportedly, take advantage of the 35% tax credits from the city and state. While it is unlikely that ABC imposed financial burdens on the cast members of this Emmy-winning show, it is always comfortable to know in advance that your contract has built-in relocation fees to help offset the costs and expenses of this type of transition.

### Payments to Loan-Out Companies
Chapter 20 discusses loan-out companies and when they make sense for your child. As for a deal point relating to loan-out companies, if your child offers his or her services through one, rather than as an individual, it is very important to negotiate a deal point that guarantees that all payments are made to the loan-out company using the company tax identification number, rather than directly to your child as an individual using her Social Security Number. This will avoid accounting and income tax problems down the road. I have known actors who operate through a loan-out company who have experienced misdirected payments and I assure you that they are difficult to undo, so a provision in the contract properly directing payments avoids all confusion on the issue.

### Guild Pension, Health & Welfare Benefits
Although producers have an obligation to make all Guild pension, health and welfare contributions *directly* to the applicable Guild, you will sleep better at night knowing that you have added this provision as a term to the contract.

### Dressing Rooms and Trailer Accommodations
Actors and actresses on both feature Film and television projects are typically afforded "on-set" dressing room accommodations and trailer accommodations while on location shoots. Dressing rooms and trailers come in a wide variety of shapes and sizes and can be equipped

with either very basic amenities, all the comforts of home, or everything in between. One of the best ways to be treated fairly when it comes to dressing rooms and trailer accommodations is to negotiate a "favored nations" clause related to this deal point.

## Per Diem

*Per diem* (Latin for "per day" or "for each day") is a daily cash allowance afforded to actors and actresses for expenses over and above all other compensation, including travel expenses and hotel accommodations on projects where the shoot location is outside your "local" area of residence. This usually means outside the general geographic county or region, typically more than seventy-five miles away from home. *Per diem* pay was first created to eliminate the need for actors to create reimbursement expense reports that would normally document the amount spent while traveling to and working on location shoots. Other than for Star actors and actresses, *per diem* allowances usually range anywhere from $50 to $75, but higher rates can be negotiated if traveling to expensive cities, especially expensive international cities, like Paris or Tokyo. The nice thing about a *per diem* is that this cash is nonrefundable, and even if it is $250 per day and your shoot location is in a jungle in South America where you can not possibly spend the money, you do not have to give back any of the "unused" money. Essentially, this amounts to another small way for you and your child to financially improve the deal.

## Personal Appearances

The specific guidelines and limitations with respect to the number of personal appearances that are required should be clearly set forth in your child's contract, beyond which additional compensation must be paid, including the amount of compensation. This includes travel costs and hotel accommodation expenses for personal appearances more than a set distance from where you live.

## DVD Copy

Producers are notorious for promising to provide actors with a copy of a DVD of any Pilot, Series, or Motion Picture, yet countless actors and actresses spend months, if not longer, chasing after one. A contractual provision that, upon the actor's request, the producer shall provide the actor with a DVD copy of any Pilot, Series or Motion Picture related to the contract will help considerably. Most producers put conditions on complying with this requirement: namely, that the actor's request must await telecast of the episode or release of the movie and that the provision only applies if the actor appears recognizably on screen. Also, they typically add a limitation that the actor can only use the material for personal, noncommercial use. Even with the limitations, this contractual provision will help you get the DVD that you were promised.

### Worker's Compensation and General Liability Insurance

To ensure your child's protection and that proper insurance coverage is in place, I recommend adding a specific provision to the contract that your child's services under the contract are: (1) subject to all applicable worker's compensation statutes of the United States, and (2) that the producer has in fact purchased both workers compensation and general liability insurance for the project which is the subject of the contract.

## FOUR DEAL POINTS THAT APPLY SPECIFICALLY TO CONTRACTS WITH CHILDREN

### Teacher Consultation Consent Guidelines Related to Minors

All employers in the entertainment business, when hiring a minor, must provide a studio teacher in accordance with Title 8 of the *California Code of Regulations*. However, a concerned parent should negotiate a deal point giving him or her the right to consult with the producer prior to the engagement of a particular studio teacher for a television Pilot/Series or Motion Picture so that you have some input as to who is selected. While consultation consents and rights are not a guarantee that your child will have a teacher who perfectly matches his or her learning personality, negotiating a key deal point helps protect against a situation in which your child and the teacher have some type of personality disconnect which might interfere with his or her ability to learn while on the set, or create some other less-than-optimum situation for your child. While most producers will make any teacher consultation consents subject to union and budgetary guidelines, and also require that final decisions are within their control, exercising some rights and input can generally be of great value to your child.

### Payment for Petition for Court Approval of Minor's Contract

Most contracts with minors contain a provision that the minor and the parents will fully cooperate with the producer on matters relating to the preparation and filing of a Petition for Approval of Minor's Contract. Savvy parents are sure to include a provision that all legal fees, court filing fees and any other related expenses are borne by and the obligation of the producer. When dealing with the major television or Motion Picture studios, it would be very rare for them to have any other expectation; however, for the avoidance of all doubt, it is best to include this provision. A provision clearly expressing to whom this obligation falls is even more important when dealing with independent or lower-budget projects.

### Coogan Trust Account Deposit Guarantee for Minors

Producers have an obligation under California and New York law (plus a small handful of other states) to make all Coogan Trust Account (sometimes called a Minor's Trust Account) deposits in the sum of 15% of a minor's gross earnings *directly* into the child's account. However, as with the above, you will sleep better at night knowing that you have added this provision as a guarantee to the contract and that this legal obligation is taken care of on your child's behalf.

### Travel and Hotel Accommodations for You and Your Child

Under the current SAG-AFTRA Union Agreements producers must provide your child *plus one parent or guardian* business-class travel, and if business class is not available, provide first-class travel. Business-class travel may be provided only if no other employee of the Producer who is represented by a guild or union is furnished a higher class of transportation on the same flight. With a few limitations that can be found in the Union Agreements, Coach-Class travel may be provided on domestic flights of less than a thousand airline miles, on non-stop flights only, measured from the departure point to the final destination point. SAG-AFTRA also requires first-class hotel accommodations (room and tax only), and reasonable ground transportation to and from airports as well as to and from the hotel and the studio or shoot location. What does all this mean? It means that if you want to be certain that you will get this type of travel and hotel accommodation, or a better class of travel or a better guarantee when it comes to travel, you must make it a deal point that you negotiate and have written into your child's contract.

## Closing Comments and Other
## Deal Points for Consideration

Keep in mind that there are other deal points which may seem in-significant at the time when one books and negotiates a project, but can become more important once on the set, and in particular as one's career advances. These include things like *audit rights,* which are very important if you are able to negotiate profit participation as part of your child's compensation package. Without adequate audit rights there will be no reasonable way for you to verify if your child is actually getting paid what he or she is entitled to be paid under the profit participation clause of the contract. Audit rights are discussed in greater detail in Chapter 27.

Other deal points that may not seem very important early on, but may become very important later on, are things like *name and likeness approvals* regarding the use of images and photographs, posters, paid ads, and related promotional materials. While it is hard to imagine that a Producer would be motivated to use a bad picture of your child, what he or she may think is perfect for conveying a certain message may differ greatly from your first-choice photograph. Therefore, if you have at least some say in "approving" such things, you are more likely to feel good about what images of your child are being used.

Additionally, as your child's career develops, getting pre-approval rights on hair and make-up professionals or, more so, getting a guar-anteed pre-approval with your favorite personal make-up and/or hair stylist, or seeking reimbursement for an on-set assistant, or determin-ing how close or far away the parking facility is from the set or your particular parking space all become deal points that you may wish to negotiate as a part of your child's contract.

Also keep in mind that some of the above deal points are very hard, if not impossible, to negotiate when your child is new in the entertain-ment business and developing his or her career. Your ability to negoti-ate many of these will depend on a number of factors, including how much the producer wants your child and how much bargaining power and clout you and your child have at the time of booking a particular project. These things come with time, experience, and success, so be cautious at first about pushing too hard on many of these later deal points. Pushing too hard could blow your child's deal.

# CHAPTER 22

## YOUR HOLLYWOOD LABOR UNIONS

*If I went to work in a factory, the first thing
I would do is join a union.*

—Franklin D. Roosevelt

It might seem like a strange detour to end a discussion of commission rates and key deal points and then turn to a discussion of labor unions. But the entertainment industry in the United States, especially in California and New York, has long been deeply influenced by labor unions. As a parent you cannot understand the financial aspects of the industry, or how your child actor gets paid, if you don't know at least the basics of how labor unions work in Hollywood.

In the world of entertainment there were, historically, two major labor unions (called Guilds) working on behalf of actors, performers, and artists—The Screen Actors Guild (SAG) and The American Federation of Television and Radio Artists (AFTRA). The term "Guild" is synonymous with "union," and simply refers to a voluntary society or fraternity of people employed in the same profession or craft who join together for the mutual protection of its members, each of whom pays a fee—a gild, for its general expenses.

## THE SCREEN ACTORS GUILD (SAG)

Historically, the Screen Actors Guild (SAG) was the nation's largest labor union representing working actors. Established in 1933, SAG had a long and rich history in the American labor movement, from standing up to studios to breaking long-term engagement contracts in the 1940s to fighting for actors' rights in the far-reaching digital revolution now impacting the entertainment industry in the 21st century.

SAG alone represented over 125,000 actors who worked in Film and digital Motion Pictures and television programs, commercials, video games, corporate/educational media, Internet and all new media formats. The Guild existed to enhance and improve actors' working conditions, maximize compensation and benefits, and to be a powerful, unified voice on behalf of actors' rights.

SAG has, of course, been equally important to both children and adults, and SAG formally recognized its obligation to children in 1975, when it formed the SAG National Young Performers Committee. Since its inception, the Committee has dealt with major issues impacting minors in show business, including lobbying to revise the *California Labor Code* as it applies to work by minors in entertainment, expanding the Coogan Laws (discussed in Chapter 26), streamlining the child's work permit process, and other important developments impacting child entertainers.

SAG operates through three main divisions: the Hollywood Division, the New York Division, and the Regional Branch Division, with twenty branches nationwide.

## THE AMERICAN FEDERATION OF TELEVISION AND RADIO ARTISTS (AFTRA)

Historically, AFTRA was a national labor union representing over 70,000 performers, journalists, and other artists working in the entertainment and news media. AFTRA's scope of representation was largely different from SAG's. It covered broadcast, public and cable television (news, sports and weather), drama and comedy, soaps, talk and variety shows, documentaries, children's programming, reality TV programming, game shows, everything radio (news, commercials, hosted programs, etc.), sound recordings (CDs, singles, Broadway cast albums, audiobooks), "non-broadcast" and industrial material, as well as Internet and digital programming.

AFTRA has also generally been more decentralized than SAG. AFTRA "locals" have always been the heart and soul of the AFTRA Guild, providing staff, services, and support in the major communities around the country where AFTRA members worked. AFTRA locals were always organized geographically: The Western Local, The Central Local, and The Eastern Local, with each having multiple offices and collectively covering the entire United States. Each local represented all categories of AFTRA membership.

## SAG–AFTRA MERGER

On March 30, 2012, members of SAG and AFTRA voted overwhelmingly to approve the merger of the two labor unions, now appropriately called SAG–AFTRA. This was a watershed event and will likely continue to have far-reaching implications not only on how actors are compensated, but also on many other issues impacting the world of entertainment. There are, however, certain aspects of the role of unions in entertainment that are unlikely to change. Chief among them is Rule One.

## RULE ONE

Check the backside of any SAG membership card, now the SAG–AFTRA card, and you'll see the most important rule by which union members, children and adults alike, must abide. It's called "Rule One" and it states that no member shall work for or agree to work for a producer who is not a signatory to an appropriate basic union agreement with the Guild. In plain language, that means that a union member must always work under a union contract, and must NEVER work non-union. This is designed to help protect actors and actresses when they work in Film, television, and commercials. In 2002, Rule One was expanded to a worldwide concept, which then became known as Global Rule One.

The importance of Rule One cannot be overstated. Entertainment is a rare industry in this country in which almost every major production is unionized, meaning that essentially every major movie production you have seen is governed by a union contract. The same is true of all network television shows and almost every major cable television channel. Likewise, performers on unionized Films virtually always make more money than those working on non-union projects.

The collective bargaining agreements that SAG and AFTRA negotiated with television studios govern a wide range of financial issues that are important to working actors of all ages. As is explained in detail in the next two chapters, these include establishing minimum pay scales for actors, as well as managing the health, pension, and other benefits that eligible actors receive.

# CHAPTER 23

## WHAT DO ACTORS EARN IN FILM, TV AND COMMERCIALS?

> *Ashley: I hope we're making two dollars a week.*
> *Mary-Kate: What, are you crazy? Two dollars? I swear if we're not*
> *making ten, I'm going home.*
>
> —Mary-Kate and Ashley Olsen

This chapter will give you a very good sense of how much money a child actor can earn for various roles in TV, Film, and commercials on projects covered by SAG–AFTRA union contracts.

However, a few words of caution are in order before we look at specific compensation and earning figures—whether for TV, Film, or commercial projects. It is very difficult to predict precisely what your child should expect to get paid in connection with a specific performance, because many factors go into determining how much is both initially offered and ultimately paid. In addition, these factors can change and evolve depending on a host of other issues that will be discussed below. You should, therefore, review this chapter to get a general idea of how compensation works in Hollywood, but keep in mind that, other than the minimum income levels, there are few clear-cut or black-and-white answers or rules.

To begin, there are a few factors that go a long way in explaining why some actors and actresses make so much more money than everyone else. The most important of these factors are experience and bargaining power—which can be, but are not always, related. The more experience an actor has, backed by a resume to prove it, the more likely he or she will book more meaningful roles, with related increased compensation. The more bargaining power the talent has, the easier it is for him/her to negotiate greater income and other perks and benefits.

No one has more bargaining power than when someone who has lots of money wants to work with a particular performer or creates a role or character specifically for that person. The term lots of money is relative, especially with respect to movies. A smaller independent production may have a budget of under $1 to $2 million, while a more richly financed Film might be produced for between $5 and $10 million or up to $25 million, whereas big-budget studio Films will often have a budget of $100 million and, in some recent cases, far more. On average, of course, the greater the budget, the more the lead and supporting actors and actresses on the project will earn.

The perception that a performer has no reasonably available substitute is the essence of bargaining power. That is why Daniel Radcliffe or Miley Cyrus can earn millions of dollars in Film and television. The movie and TV studios know very well that their huge fan base and on-screen charisma and presence compel audiences to watch them, and with that come increased box-office sales at the theaters and increased viewer ratings on television. Few people are perceived to have that bargaining power. And so, if you want Daniel Radcliffe to Star in your movie or Miley Cyrus to be the series lead on your TV show, there is only one of them available. That's why they have a huge amount of bargaining power and that will continue until they are perceived as unable to attract audiences.

However, Hollywood perceives the vast majority of actors to be replaceable. This is particularly true when actors first start working in the entertainment industry. This explains why, for example, producers offer an unknown actress a lot less money to appear in a new TV show than they will when the show becomes a hit. Once the show starts making lots of money, the stars or Series Regulars appearing on that show have much more bargaining power than they had at the outset. That is why, for example, Ariel Winter, Rico Rodriguez, and Nolan Gould, the children on the hit television show *Modern Family,* were reportedly able to negotiate substantially better salaries after the show won Emmy Awards, Golden Globe Awards, and Teen Choice Awards in back-to-back seasons. When the show became a hit, the adult and child stars of that show became closely identified with the show, and they were perceived to be irreplaceable. In short, they had bargaining power.

The other factor that helps explain why compensation in Hollywood varies as much as it does is the level of involvement a particular performer has in a project. Generally speaking, and all other things being equal, people whose performance requires more time on set (e.g., weeks shooting a Motion Picture as compared to days) earn more money. Likewise, an actor who appears in all the episodes of a TV show (commonly called All Shows Produced and abbreviated ASP) earns more money per episode than someone who appears in 6 of every 13 episodes.

However, there are times when bargaining power can, with respect to compensation, override the importance of role size. For example, sometimes a TV network will pay more for a 3-day Guest Star appearance on a TV show than the weekly compensation of some of its Series Regulars on that same show, if the actor doing the Guest Star spot has huge bargaining power. The same concept holds true in movies. For example, Jack Nicholson is reported to have made millions for shooting a limited role as The Joker in the 1989 *Batman* movie, which reportedly grossed $413 million worldwide, but only cost $35 million to produce. Again, that's a situation where someone was asked for by name, so one might be wise to assume he also participated in the overall profits of the Film. Whatever the details may have been, we know that, as a three-time Oscar-winning actor, Jack Nicholson had, and still has, a lot of bargaining-power.

Now that you understand the importance of experience, bargaining power, and a variety of other variables, we can now specifically turn to how much children and young adults earn in television.

## COMPENSATION FOR CHILDREN AND YOUNG ADULTS IN TELEVISION

The payment schedules discussed in the remainder of this chapter were established by SAG before the SAG-AFTRA merger of March 20, 2012 (discussed in Chapter 22), but are, of course, still valid following the merger, you will see references to both SAG and SAG/AFTRA, depending on the context of the discussion.

### Union Minimum Pay (Television)
The union contract that was most recently negotiated by the Screen Actors Guild includes minimum pay scales for a wide array of actors (i.e., Day Performers, Stunt Performers, Background Performers, etc.). In June 2009, after a protracted nine-month labor dispute between the Hollywood studios and the Screen Actors Guild, a new two-year contract was ratified by 78% of the approximately 40,000 SAG members who voted. That Agreement, as amended by memoranda dated 2011, is the source of many of the minimum compensation rates that follow. The minimum rates listed in this and the following chapters became effective June 1, 2012. Under the SAG-AFTRA contracts, the minimum rates described below are effective from June 1, 2013, for the one-year period through June 30, 2014.

For a TV Guest Star, the minimum rate depends in part on whether the actor is guaranteed the 5-day minimum rate or books an 8-day engagement. The 5-day guarantee shown below applies to half-hour television (usually a comedy), and the longer 8-day rate applies to one-hour television (usually a dramatic series).

**Minimum Union Pay Scale**
**(Television Guest Star)**

Guest Star Role
(aka Major Role Performer)
for half-hour television.............. $4,890 for five days

Guest Star Role
(aka Major Role Performer)
for one-hour television............. $7,823 for eight days

### Recurring and Series Regular Roles on TV

By almost everyone's standards, as shown above, even unknown actors and actresses make a lot of money when they appear on television shows. The exact amount depends on factors such as the network involved (whether a major network or cable station), the number of episodes in which the talent will perform under contract, and whether there is a guarantee that the actor or actress will appear in a certain minimum number of episodes.

Recurring Roles and Series Regular roles can result in even more dramatic compensation for those who worked hard to achieve that level of success. The figures below assume that an actor or actress has a significant role on a particular show. The highest compensation rates go to Series Regulars—those who appear in every, or virtually every, episode. The next most highly compensated actors appear in Recurring Roles. As the name suggests, they appear more than one time, and some appear many times over multiple seasons, as when my client, Lou Ferrigno, appeared in a Recurring Role of between three and six times per season on CBS's hit comedy *King of Queens*. As one would expect, while the recurring compensation can be significant for someone like *The Hulk*, unknown actors who recur or appear on a single episode, or who are background performers (commonly called extras), get paid much less.

As a general rule, if your child books a TV Pilot, which simply refers to the first episode of a television series, the potential then exists for your child to be offered a per-episode rate of between $5,000 and $15,000 and possibly more, to appear in a Series Regular role on that TV Pilot. Thus, it is not unusual for the "episodic compensation" for Series Regulars who appear on a television show on a major network to be on the higher side of the range, meaning between $7,500 and $15,000 per episode or more, with compensation for cable TV likely fluctuating more, and tending, of course, to be on the lower end of the range. Given that a typical primetime network show will schedule twenty-two episodes per season (twenty-three including the Pilot), you can quickly see that appearing on TV pays a whole lot more than babysitting, or working at a restaurant or any retail store in a local mall.

That said, and because the above compensation figures are not guaranteed, here are some examples of SAG-AFTRA minimum rates for a Series Regular role:

**Minimum Union Pay Scale**
(Television Recurring Series Regular Role)
For a Recurring Series Regular Role (one in which the actor is guaranteed to appear in a minimum of at least six episodes), the SAG minimums are as follows, effective July 1, 2013:

Contract Guaranteeing Minimum
of Six half-hour Episodes......................$4,116 per week

Contract Guaranteeing Minimum
of Six one-hour Episodes......................$4,839 per week

### Residual Income and Merchandising Royalty Income for Television

When a show is re-broadcast, all actors and actresses appearing as Day Players, Guest Stars, and, of course, Series Regulars receive Rerun royalty payments, commonly called Residuals. The amount of the Residual depends on how often the show is re-broadcast. The SAG-AFTRA contract sets forth the following minimum payments:

| **Union Minimum Residuals** |
| :---: |
| **(Television)** |

First Rerun of a half-hour
Television Network Prime Time..................... $2,428

First Rerun of a one-hour
Television Network Prime Time..................... $3,456

## CASE STUDY

### ERIN MORAN ON HAPPY DAYS

*The basic per-episode structure for compensation on TV has existed for a long time. In the 1970s, before cable TV existed, ABC had a new show that later became an enormous syndicated hit— Happy Days. The young actress who played Joanie on that show, Erin Moran, entered into a six-year Test Option/Series Contract in 1973. She was twelve years old at the time and was paid $650 per episode for the first year, $750 for the second, and $900 for the third. Although the per-episode amounts paid today are much higher, the basic structure of the Test Option/Series Option has remained fairly consistent. The details of Erin Moran's 1973 contract became public a few years ago, when she sued ABC for allegedly failing to properly pay her residuals income.*

The residual income rates for the second through fifth repeat are calculated on a downward sliding scale of 50% to 25% of the current first rerun minimum. Foreign broadcast residuals are calculated using separate formulas.

In addition to the above, compensation for Series Regular roles can often include an additional "merchandising royalty." Typically, the royalty payment is 5% of net profits earned for merchandise produced and sold that is related to the show, or, in particular, "your character" on the show. These variations in the potential compensation ultimately negotiated depend on a variety of factors, including the network involved, whether it is a major network show or cable network, the type of show, and how effective your agent or attorney is at closing a favorable deal.

### Television Syndication

You may have seen television shows celebrate the filming of their 100th episode. Yes, 100 is a magical number in television, and the broadcasting or airing of that many episodes is quite an achievement. Very few television shows make it that far.

There is, however, another reason why the actors and actresses are smiling so broadly during the 100th-episode party. Once a show has aired 100 episodes, it can be "syndicated." Syndication, by definition, refers to the sale of a series of television programs directly to local TV stations in the U.S. and around the world. Once sold, the shows can be aired 24/7 and seen on a variety of networks. Financially, syndication of television programs is often a goldmine. When a TV show goes into syndication, actors have the opportunity to earn residual income every time an episode in which they appeared is aired, and this can be one of the more lucrative ways that TV actors get paid long after they have stopped working on set. Some shows have been in syndication for decades, and some actors and actresses have been receiving residual income from those shows for many years after they stopped performing a particular role.

### Common Misconceptions About Per-Episode Compensation

Many people starting out draw the wrong conclusions when they see how much television pays per episode, thinking that's where the big money is. While a child's per-episode compensation is significant, the more important long-term factor in determining whether your child will earn significant dollars by landing a leading role on television is whether the show is a hit. Many pilots are filmed but never air. Others are filmed and air, but don't survive a single full season. Thus, for example, if a show is cancelled after four episodes (which is often when networks decide to pull shows with disappointing viewer ratings), the actor only gets paid for those four episodes plus any other episodes actually shot, but not yet aired.

So what's the best strategy for making a lot of money as a child in television? Do everything you can to make the show a success. In other words, be professional and a good team player, and get along with the other people on the show (both in front of and behind the camera), prepare well, and by all means do your best work and give it your all. If you do that, and you are fortunate enough to be on a show that becomes a hit, you'll not only have more fun you should have some bargaining power and command a much higher per-episode compensation rate than you did for your initial contract.

Too many parents and children sabotage their careers in entertainment by failing to understand how important it is to work hard, get along with others, and still be on the show when it becomes a hit.

### *The Initial "Test Option" Contract*

When you book a Pilot, you will be asked to sign a multi-year Test Option Contract, which typically has fairly modest built-in pay increases. Specifically, it's common to be asked (if not required) to sign a six-series-year option for a Fall Season start (equivalent to 22–23 episodes), or a six-and-a-half series year option for a mid-season start contract with 5% increases (bumps) in compensation at the start of each series year. As such, negotiating solid and fair compensation for series year one *actually impacts the entire term,* because the compensation for future series years that will hopefully follow is first based on the Year-One rate.

Thus, when a Test Option/Series Contract is first presented to you, you should retain an experienced entertainment lawyer to negotiate on your behalf. In fact, given the expectation in terms of negotiating compensation as well as many other factors, common sense demands it. These contracts are complicated and cover long periods of time, so you will want to make sure that you understand your contract, and that it serves your child well, and that he or she is being compensated and otherwise treated fairly. When you fi rst start in entertainment, and when no one knows

**CASE STUDY**

*Early in 2013, also known in the entertainment industry as Pilot Season 2013, during the editing process of this book, I received a telephone call from Justin and Laura Ward, the parents of the very talented, up-and-coming young, actor, Mateus Ward. Mateus had just been informed that his recent auditioning was admired and that he was being brought in for a Studio Test for a Series Regular role by Warner Brothers producers for a "Studio Test" on a new Jerry Bruckheimer TV Pilot. We all knew what that meant. Mateus' lengthy "Agreement for Test with Pilot and Series Options" had to be reviewed, completely negotiated, and signed within (in this case) 48 hours—or he would not be considered by the Studio or the Network producers as one of the four finalists for the role. Long before that telephone call from WB, Mateus' parents anticipated this day could come so both his Talent Agent, Jennifer Patredis, a super agent from Innovated Artists, and I were ready on a moment's notice. We brainstormed, consulted, took care of business, and closed the deal in a timely manner. The next day, Mateus booked the role and is on location shooting the Pilot as I type these words. In short, the Ward family was prepared, and success happens when opportunity and preparation meet.*

you by name, it's hard to negotiate compensation and other terms unless you have someone experienced in such matters at your side and protecting your interests. Television studios have experienced legal and business affairs personnel (usually attorneys) on their side—you must level the playing field by doing the same for your child.

## How Much Do Actors Earn on Motion Pictures?

The compensation structure for a feature Film or Motion Picture is different from that of a TV series. Depending on the role, television compensation is often based on daily, 5-day, 8-day, or weekly compensation rates, because one episode of most shows is shot in a week. By contrast, Films normally take weeks or months to shoot, and performers are paid a flat fee for the entire Film, especially if they are big-budget pictures shot at various locations around the world and produced by one of the big studios.

As in TV, you get paid more on average the bigger your role. For example, a lead role in a Motion Picture might be involved in twenty or more days of shooting. Someone with a more minor role may only be needed for a few days or one week. The lead might therefore be paid a single flat fee for the entire production. But the supporting actor might be paid for a single week, and someone with a more minor role may be paid on a daily basis.

Because movie budgets vary tremendously, so too does the compensation. A lead role on a Major Motion Picture (made and distributed by a large studio) might pay between $25,000 and $100,000 or more for the entire production. The supporting actors might earn $5,000 for a single week's shooting. An independent Film, by contrast, would almost certainly pay much less.

---

**Union Minimum Pay for Movies**

The SAG-AFTRA agreement includes the following minimum rates for movie actors, effective July 1, 2013:

Minimum Pay Scale (Movies)

Day Player (one-day speaking part in a movie):. . . . . . $859/day
Weekly Performer Rate (movie): . . . . . . . . . . . . . . $2,979/week

*The figures described above are union-negotiated minimums.*

---

These figures obviously don't apply to huge stars like Daniel Radcliffe,

Star of the Harry Potter movie franchise, or Vanessa Hudgens, one of the young leading cast members of the highly successful *High School Musical* franchise. How do they get paid? Unlike TV shows, Films don't generate residual income in the same sense of the term. Films generate ongoing streams of income through sophisticated "back-end profit-participation" deals, the terms of which are dependent on the success of the Film, merchandise and other related ancillary sources. It is therefore difficult to generalize; contracts are negotiated on a role-by-role basis, Film-by-Film basis, or when an actor may be fortunate enough to sign a multi-Film deal with a particular studio.

In general, however, it is safe to say that the highest-paid Film roles feature some combination of a large upfront payment, as well as a "back-end profit-participation" fee based on a percentage of the net earnings of the Film and sales of related merchandise and products. For franchises like *Harry Potter* and *The Hunger Games*, the highest potential compensation may actually come from getting a percentage of the box office sales, merchandise sales, and profits. This is perhaps the most common way in which Film actors of all ages can earn significant dollars, if not, in some cases, millions of dollars for a single Film.

To put Film compensation in perspective, most actors strive to break the union minimums. These minimums come primarily from what performers earn from their on-set performance. Thus, the best way for most young performers to make money in Film is for them to get increasingly more prominent roles in movies with larger budgets. However, your child can still have a lot of fun and earn good income even if he or she doesn't become the next break-out Star or a worldwide phenomenon.

## COMPENSATION FOR TV COMMERCIALS

Many actors and actresses choose to start their careers by appearing in commercials. There are significantly more opportunities to appear in a "principal role" in a commercial than on a TV series or feature Film.

Two factors help determine how much children are paid to appear on a television commercial: (1) how often the commercial is shown; and (2) the scope of its distribution. The more often the commercial is seen, the more the actors appearing in it get paid. Likewise, commercials that are aired for nationwide distribution pay more—and sometimes much more—than regional or local commercials. There can also be large differences between local and regional markets, which tend to track the number of people living in those markets. Generally speaking, the more eyeballs in the market, the higher the average compensation. With all of these factors in play, it can be difficult to give precise compensation for television commercials, but this next section will give you a great roadmap for understanding compensation for children in union television commercials.

The initial way in which actors get paid for commercials is what they receive to actually shoot the commercial, called a Session Fee. Most commercials are usually shot in a day or two, which means an actor will normally earn a one-day or two-day Session Fee for shooting the commercial. Once the commercial is shot, most of the money earned in SAG-AFTRA television commercials is derived from residual income.

### Minimum Pay for TV Commercials

The SAG 2009 Commercial Contract (negotiated before the SAG-AFTRA merger), which is still in effect, explains all of the compensation rates for an actor performing in a union commercial. Under the Agreement, the minimum Session Fee (fee for shooting the commercial) for a principal on-camera actor for a Class "A" commercial is $592.20 per day. A Class "A" commercial is essentially defined as "network broadcast use." If a commercial is running on interconnected stations (a network) in more than 21 cities, or sponsors a program ("This program is brought to you by ..."), it also constitutes a Class "A" commercial.

Other rates paid to actors vary for things like Group Spots, Class "C" Commercials, Internet Spots, Crowd Scenes, and a variety of other uses, such as Industrial Use Commercials, Public Service Announcements (PSAs), and Non-Air Demos, which pay lesser rates. Minimum rates for Internet spots also went into effect, as of April 1, 2011.

As always, top "A" list lead actors and actresses, and even those who are well known but may not quite be in that "A" List category, can negotiate far more than the mandated minimums set forth in the union contract.

### Residual Income from TV Commercials

As indicated above, the real money in commercials is made from Residual Income when the commercial plays over and over again, day after day. Before it goes off the air, the average national Class "A" commercial generates around $10,000 in total gross income. I know actors who have seen a single commercial generate $35,000 in a year, and I have personally had a few clients generate $75,000 to $100,000 on a single spot over the course of about 18 to 24 months, although these larger amounts are less common than they used to be.

Additionally, if the producer wishes to retain the rights to air the commercial and wants to "hold" a performer exclusive to the product, the producer must pay the performer Holding Fees in fixed 13-week cycles. During this 13-week period, a performer cannot accept work in a commercial for a competitive product. For example, if a performer has received a holding fee for a Pepsi commercial, he/she may not accept work for a commercial advertising Coca-Cola during that period of time.

Now let's discuss some little-known rules. The first is that the "maximum period of use" of a commercial is 21 months (a total of seven 13-week holding-fee cycles). Provided the producer continues to make timely holding-fee payments, the performer may not appear in a commercial for a competitor for the entire 21-month period. If the performer (or his/her representative) does not send a timely "renegotiation letter," the commercial's producer can extend the maximum period of use for an additional 21 months *at the same rates.*

Next, if the performer wants to preserve the right to negotiate higher rates at the end of the 21-month cycle, a renegotiation letter must be sent 60 to 120 days (two to four months) prior to the end of the maximum period of use. The letter should be sent to the producer (ad agency) listed on the employment contract. Sending the letter gives the performer's agent the right to renegotiate new rates or to say he/she does not grant the right to continued use of the commercial. Performers should at the same time also send a copy of the letter to the Screen Actors Guild. If the Talent Agent does not send a renegotiation letter, and the commercial is renewed for an additional 21 months at the minimum scale rate, the agent may not take a commission.

Commercials that go through the renegotiation process almost always generate a very nice increase in compensation. As a result of the higher rates and number of times such commercials are aired, renegotiated TV commercial contracts may pay a single performer more than $100,000.

There is also a very special type of commercial, called a Commercial Campaign, which is essentially an advanced form of a long-term commercial commitment by an advertiser. Commercial Campaigns have been known to generate very substantial income streams for performers ranging from already famous talent (e.g., Catherine Zeta Jones/T-Mobile Campaign), to the somewhat well-known (Carly Foulkes/T-Mobile Pink Girl on Motorcycle Campaign), and, of course, the totally unknown ("Can you hear me now?"/Verizon Guy Campaign), to "Flo" the quirky upbeat Progressive Insurance employee who has now appeared in over 50 commercials, and as of December 2013 has over one million fans and has generated more than 5.3 million "likes" on Facebook. For those actors fortunate enough to be featured in a high-profile Commercial Campaign, the resulting income streams have been reported to exceed one million dollars.

## THE BOTTOM LINE ABOUT HOLLYWOOD PAY

So what's the basic message of how people get really rich in entertainment? Work hard, do a great job, get along with people—and stick around long enough to be able to renegotiate your initial contract, or book a project that leverages your existing project. In other words, position yourself so that you have enough of a name that you can negotiate a higher–paying contract for a new television show, commercial, or Major Motion Picture.

Contrary to what too many parents and children in Hollywood believe, working hard, training hard, doing a good job, getting along with others, and contributing to a hit show or blockbuster movie is the best way to earn top dollars. Likewise, being a high-maintenance problematic actor or actress is often the quickest way to derail your career and leave lots of money on the table.

*I'm just so thrilled to have dental!*
—Anne Hathaway in her SAG Awards Acceptance Speech, 2013

Many performers receive health insurance and other benefits under the terms of the union contracts that have been negotiated by SAG–AFTRA. Specifically, these contracts provide health and pension benefits, as well as life insurance. The health insurance includes coverage for Major Medical, Dental, and Vision. Pension benefits consist of programs for regular pensions, early retirement pensions, disability pensions, and related benefits.

Whether an actor or actress receives these benefits, and the extent of coverage the benefits provide, depends on two factors: (1) the amount an actor earns from producers who signed the union contract (called Union signatories), and (2) the timely payment of a premium by the actor.

## HEALTH INSURANCE COVERAGE UNDER THE SAG CONTRACT

The best way to understand how benefits under the union contracts work is to review the SAG Health Plan. It has two levels of medical benefits, Plan I and Plan II, both through Blue Cross, as well as Delta Dental PPO coverage, and the Exam Plus Plan for vision.

To receive health insurance under either Plan I or II, you have to earn a minimum amount of money over a twelve-month period, or work more than a minimum number of days during the year. Plan I provides better coverage than Plan II. For 2013, the minimum-earnings requirement for Plan I is, therefore, about twice as high as for Plan II:

### SAG Health Plan: Minimum Yearly Earning Requirement
Plan I:  $30,750
Plan II:  $15,100 (or 76 days of covered employment)

These minimum requirements are expected to increase by an estimated

3% per year. The increase, if any, will be determined by the people who act as trustees for the Plan, based on an annual review of the Health Plan's financial condition.

The biggest challenge for most actors is to earn enough money in a single year to be eligible to receive health coverage under either Plan I or II. Once an actor earns the minimum amount in any twelve-month period, he is eligible to receive health benefits. The exact date in which you receive benefits depends on when during the year you hit the minimum earnings threshold. Generally speaking, if you hit the minimum earnings threshold in a particular quarter, you can begin to receive health benefits three months later. For example, if you hit the minimum income threshold in the quarter ending December 31, your health insurance coverage will begin the following April.

## Premiums

As with any insurance coverage, you have to pay premiums. Under the SAG Health Plan, participants are required to pay a quarterly premium. The premium structure allows participants to choose a rate based on the number of dependents they elect to cover under the Plan. For example, the quarterly premium for one participant is $273 for Plan I, and $324 for Plan II.

Given that SAG had more than 125,000 members, and AFTRA over 70,000 members it isn't surprising that they are able to negotiate good group insurance rates. In light of the merger between SAG and AFTRA, and the importance that actors place on benefits in general and health insurance in particular, it is likely that the actors who earn enough to meet the requirements of Plan I will continue to receive very good health coverage at relatively affordable rates.

Although many children in entertainment are covered by their parents' health insurance policies, a sizeable percentage of parents lack health insurance or would like to have their children covered by higher-quality health insurance. Children who earn more than the annual yearly minimums provided for in the union contracts can obtain such coverage. It is an additional potential benefit of being a successful entertainment kid.

## How the Merger of SAG and AFTRA Impacted Health Insurance and Retirement Plans

According to a Press Release issued by SAG-AFTRA and posted on the new website, The SAG-AFTRA National Board voted overwhelmingly (99.47%) to approve a motion urging the union and industry trustees of the SAG Producers Pension and Health Plans ("P&H") and the AFTRA Health & Retirement Funds (H&R) to undertake expeditious and appropriate action to create a unified Health Plan for performers, broadcasters and others working under SAG-AFTRA collective-bargaining agreements, and to implement immediately a reciprocity agreement between the two existing Health Plans.

The Board also urged the Plan Trustees to review the feasibility and advisability of creating a unified Defined Benefit Retirement Plan and reciprocity agreement between the existing Pension and Retirement Plans.

In light of these decisions, you can expect that, in the future, a single unified health plan will cover all performers who receive union benefits.

*The trick is to stop thinking of it as "your" money.*

—IRS Auditor

Let's now move to an important financial issue that relates to your in-teractions with Talent Agents and Talent Managers.

Talent Managers and Talent Agents incur expenses such as over-night delivery services, an occasional messenger, and sometimes even travel costs. The more active your child's career, the more costs and expenses the Talent Agent and Talent Manager are likely to generate. Someone has to pay for these costs, which is why the contract you will be asked to sign will include language describing when you need to pay for or advance costs.

The key issue here is not so much the fact that cost advances and expenses are a necessary part of representation, but rather, that you know: (1) what the expensed items will be, and (2) exactly under what circumstances you or your child will be responsible for reimbursing your child's Talent Agent or Talent Manager. These costs can add up, so it's imperative that you know what to expect and budget accord-ingly. A contract should clearly set forth some guidelines as to when the manager is required to have a particular expense pre-approved by the parent, and when he or she can simply move forward and incur an expense and simply bill the parent later.

Here are two sample provisions of how the issue of costs and ex-penses can be handled, and what to look out of for:

The first says the manager must try to contact the parent each time he incurs a cost over $50 (an amount that can, of course, vary from contract to contract):

*All reasonable and customary expenses incurred by Manager on Artist's behalf including, without limitation, duplication of pho-tographs, scripts, DVDs, CDs, overnight courier and/or messen-ger expenses shall be paid by Artist and Parent or reimbursed by Artist and Parent if Manager initially advances the funds for said expenses. If Manager is seeking to further Artist's career, but can-*

*not reach Parent or Artist within a reasonable period of time re-*
*garding an expense under $50.00 per occurrence, Manager may*
*authorize the expense on Artist and Parent's behalf. Manager*
*is authorized to deduct such reimbursable costs from any Gross*
*Earnings received by Manager on behalf of Artist and/or Parent.*
*In the event Manager is required to travel outside of Los Angeles*
*County, California on business for Artist, and Artist or Parent pre-*
*approves such travel, Artist and Parent shall pay and/or reimburse*
*Manager for Manager's reasonable expenses, including hotel, trav-*
*el and living costs in connection therewith.*

While the above provision gives the parent a lot of control and certainly helps parents monitor costs very closely, it just might be asking
too much of a manager to get in touch every time he needs to send
something out for your child. An easy way to make this provision more
reasonable would be to increase the dollar figure from, let's say, $50
to $75 or $100. You can also start the contract at a lower figure and, if
all is going well after several months, increase the figure to something
higher, yet still within your comfort zone.

The example below gives the Talent Manager more freedom to incur expenses without obtaining parental pre-approval. This approach
may be more efficient, but it also increases the chances that you will
worry about or regret how your child's money is being spent.

*All reasonable and customary expenses incurred by Manager on*
*Artist's behalf including, without limitation, duplication of pho-*
*tographs, scripts, DVDs, CDs, overnight courier and/or messen-*
*ger expenses shall be paid by Artist and Parent or reimbursed by*
*Artist and Parent if Manager initially advances the funds for said*
*expenses.*

*Manager is not required to make any loans or advances to Artist,*
*and, if such are made, they will be reimbursed immediately or*
*Manager may deduct those loans or advances from funds received*
*by Manager on Artist's behalf.*

*Manager may travel or meet with third parties on behalf of Artist*
*and Parent at Manager's discretion. If Manager travels at Artist*
*and/or Parent's request, then Manager may make such arrange-*
*ments and accommodations as Manager elects and the cost of such*
*travel will be borne by Artist and Parent.*

*Manager is authorized to deduct such reimbursable costs from any Gross Earnings received by Manager on behalf of Artist and/or Parent.*

**ROBERT'S RECOMMENDATION AND WARNING:** To work effectively for your child, a Talent Agent or Talent Manager needs latitude to incur reasonable reimbursable costs without having to get permission at every turn. However, parents should not give unfettered rights to someone whom they've just retained and allow him to incur any cost at any time. Doing that is simply too risky and exposes you and your child to what may turn out to be unnecessary costs and expenses. Until a sense of trust has developed, and the manager has established a record of good judgment, I suggest a contract provision that says that all costs over a certain predetermined amount, (whether $25, $50, or $100), must be pre-approved. This gives your child's representatives some day-to-day leeway to get things done, yet still offers you and your child protection, making it fair and reasonable for everyone. I would recommend you insist on a cost provision with a pre-approval threshold.

Additionally, the cost provision of the contract should obligate the manager to send monthly, or periodic, statements listing all ongoing expenses. You will note that each of the above examples did not contain such language. These statements should be required whether or not income is coming in from booked projects. This will help prevent surprises—even surprises that relate to the smaller costs and expenses. When children are first starting out in the business, they may net several hundred dollars from a job (after deducting commissions, Coogan Trust deposits, and taxes). You should, therefore, get into the habit of receiving and reviewing expense statements, even for relatively small amounts.

# CHAPTER 26

## WHO GETS PAID FIRST?

*While money can't buy happiness,*
*it certainly lets you choose your own form of misery.*

—Groucho Marx

As a parent, you need to know more than just how much your child may earn and what expenses you are required to pay. In short, you will be in a better position to protect your child if you also understand cash flow.

Let's assume that your son or daughter is hired to do a TV commercial. Once the money is paid, where does it go?

Who typically gets paid first?

- Child Actor
- Parents
- Talent Manager
- Talent Agent
- Entertainment Attorney

The answer is: It depends.

Now let me tell you why and what you can do about it.

Before your child or anyone else nets any money from performing as an actor, certain built-in financial obligations and costs must be deducted off the top, either by operation of law or under the terms of one or more contracts that you have signed. I'm neither a tax advisor nor tax accountant, but theres one thing I know for sure: whether we like it or not, we'll have to pay taxes and likely so will your child.

But paying taxes on a child's acting income can be a little trickier than paying taxes on income earned by adult actors or from more traditional employment income. That means you should consult with a tax professional to make sure that the proper amounts are either withheld when earned income is paid, or funds are set aside from your child's income to handle tax obligations. For some, the failure to address these obligations has been the source of enormous grief, additional expense, stress, and unwanted dealings with the Internal Revenue Service.

Additionally, before anyone else is paid, production companies and advertisers in California, New York, and a very small but growing handful of other states, are legally obligated to honor what have commonly become known as the Coogan Laws. These laws require production companies to deduct 15% of the child's gross earnings (i.e., earnings before taxes) and deposit that money *directly* into a specially qualified blocked trust account (officially called a Coogan Trust Account in California and, in New York, a Child Performer's Trust Account). Without a court order, the money in this account cannot be touched by anyone other than the child, including the child's parents. Courts rarely permit parents or others to withdraw money from Coogan Trust Accounts. Your child may freely access funds from his/her Coogan Trust Account when he or she reaches eighteen years of age. At that age, children reach what the law describes as the *age of majority*. They are legally adults, and the funds in the Coogan Trust Accounts are released to them.

Next in line to be paid are the actor's Talent Agent and Talent Manager (and, in some cases, an entertainment attorney). They receive their agreed-upon commission, calculated against the child's gross earnings (i.e., against earnings before taxes or Coogan account deductions).

What remains is often considered by many parents to be just a fraction of the child's original gross earnings from the Film, TV or commercial project. With taxes being paid off the top, the Coogan savings deduction of 15%, the manager's commission of 15%, and the agency commission of 10%, some 50% or more of your child's original earnings, may seem to "disappear." This is another reason why it is critical for parents to examine scrupulously the terms and provisions of any talent contract that they are asked to sign.

## WHERE DO THE CHECKS GO?

Most Talent Agents and Talent Managers are uncomfortable with having the child's earnings going directly to the child or child's parents—and although exceptions have been made involving well-known actors and star-name talent, they generally will not permit it. Quite simply, agents and managers fear they'll end up chasing people around for their commissions; personal past experiences and war stories from colleagues justify this concern. As a result, agents and managers often insert payment instructions into their contract. The following two sample contract provisions address very different payment instructions—and the differences are important.

When you sign with a Talent Manager *only* (i.e., you don't yet have a Talent Agent), the order in which funds are distributed is fairly straightforward. He or she receives the check, takes out his/her 15% commission, and then sends the remainder to you or your child. The situation gets a bit more complicated when an agent and a manager are both in the picture. Who should get paid first between the two of them?

The first example, below, says the manager is to receive all compensation, which he shall promptly disburse to the actor (and agent, if there is one), keeping only his commission and reimbursement of any authorized expenses:

> *All Gross Earnings payable to Artist and/or Parent shall be paid to Artist and/or Parent through Manager's Talent Trust Account. Manager shall deduct commissions and any other monies due Manager and disperse balance promptly to Artist and/or Parent's address set forth above, unless notified otherwise in writing. The commission due and payable to Artist and received by Manager shall be forwarded by Manager to Artist within five (5) business days after Manager's receipt thereof. Artist or Parent shall not at any time during this Agreement, or after the term of this Agreement has expired, engage in any action to divert receipt of payments or compensation due under the terms of this Agreement from being transmitted to Manager and paid through Manager's Talent Trust Account. The commission due and payable to Manager hereunder on any and all Gross Earnings inadvertently received directly by Artist shall be forwarded by Artist to Manager within five (5) business days after Artist's receipt thereof.*

**ROBERT'S RECOMMENDATIONS:** My primary concern with the above paragraph is that it may create a conflict with your agent's internal business policy and practices. If you're still looking for an agent, it may discourage an agency from representing your child. In other words, the above paragraph may be just fine when you only sign with a manager, but may cause problems down the road, when your child is represented by a Talent Manager and a Talent Agent. I would therefore make sure to include language that alters the disbursement of funds to fit the agent's requirements once an agent is secured for your child.

The best way to address the order in which your child's representatives get paid is to anticipate that at some point in the future you will be represented by both a Talent Manager and a Talent Agent. The following provision is useful because it resolves any potential conflict between the Talent Manager and Talent Agent by giving the Talent Agent priority. I much prefer something like this:

*Artist shall notify and irrevocably direct all third parties that are obligated to pay any Gross Earnings to or on behalf of Artist to pay such sums directly to Manager unless Artist has a Talent Agent, then all monies shall be forwarded directly to Artist's Agent, who shall then pay Manager, who in turn shall pay Artist. The commission due and payable to Artist and received by Manager shall be forwarded by Manager to Artist within five (5) business days after Manager's receipt thereof. The commission due and payable to Manager hereunder on any and all Gross Earnings inadvertently received directly by Artist shall be forwarded by Artist to Manager within five (5) business days after Artist's receipt thereof.*

Yes, it can be an eye-opening experience to see a quarter of the gross amount your child has earned go straight to his/her Talent Agent and Talent Manager, and I often hear complaints about these fees. However, as you already know, these folks are indispensable to helping your child on his/her road to fame. More importantly, please don't lose sight of the fact that it is better to pay Talent Managers and Talent Agents than not to pay them. Paying them is a sign that your child is actually a working actor or otherwise performing. I have told many clients to THINK BIG and yearn for the day they pay their agents and managers a combined $500,000, because that means they have earned two million dollars! Financially speaking, that is, after all, what you and your child want, right?

# CHAPTER 27
## UNDERSTANDING AUDIT RIGHTS

*There's no business like show business,*
*but there are several businesses like accounting.*

—David Letterman

It's one thing to feel that your child has been properly paid; it's much better to be able to demand proof of it. That's what the right to perform an audit or inspect records is all about.

An audit is a formal examination of an individual's or organization's accounting records, financial situation, or compliance with a contract. Include Audit Rights in your Talent Agent or talent management contract, or it'll be very difficult to determine if your child is being paid the right amount of money. Without having these rights built into your contract, you must either take your agent's or manager's word on what the accounting records say, consult with SAG-AFTRA for union projects, or start an expensive and time-consuming lawsuit, which will grant you subpoena power to obtain copies of those records.

Audit Rights are showing up in more and more talent contracts. Generally, this is a good thing. The specific language of the Audit Rights paragraph must be reviewed, however, to make sure it's not one-sided. Too many contracts pop up these days that give your Talent Manager Audit Rights without giving reciprocal rights to you. In short, the key to the Audit Rights provision is mutuality, meaning the obligations are reciprocal—that the obligations are mutual. Here's an example of mutual audit rights in a management contract:

> *Artist and Manager shall each have the right to conduct an audit of the other party's books and records to ensure faithful compliance with the terms of this Talent Management Agreement. Artist and Manager shall each have the right to obtain copies of all contracts, engagement letters, checks, payment vouchers, invoices and related documents, whether created as a hard copy or an electronic version, including all documents and writings that are supportive of any gross income, net earnings, all disbursements therefrom, including, but not limited, to costs and/or expenses related to the*

*terms and conditions of this Agreement. Artist and Manager shall have equal, mutual, and reciprocal rights with respect to the provisions herein, including the right to copy all necessary records to ensure the accuracy of the audit.*

As a parent, you should request audit rights in your talent contracts. When Talent Agents and Managers know that you have audit rights built into your contracts, they are much more likely to be scrupulously honest and fair when dealing with you.

Audit Rights have their limitations, however. Just because you have the right to request an audit of a Talent Manager's financial records relating to your child, doesn't mean that you should, or that it makes financial sense to do so. As indicated below, many contracts require that audits be conducted by Certified Public Accountants or other certified financial professionals.

*Audit Rights, as defined herein, may be exercised by engaging a professional entertainment industry auditor and/or a certified public accountant whose name, address and telephone number shall be provided by the requesting party to the responding party no less than 21 calendar days before the date of the audit. Audit Rights may be exercised no more than two times per any given twelve-month period and shall be limited to the three fiscal years preceding the audit, unless the audit establishes that more than $5000 is due to the auditing party, in which case the audit rights shall reach back to the commencement of the talent-artist relationship.*

CPAs and other auditors don't work for free. They typically charge hundreds of dollars per hour for their services and require a substantial initial payment (or retainer) to start their work. Therefore, it often will not make sense for you to hire auditors, unless the amount that is disputed with the Talent Agent or Talent Manager is much larger than the auditor's fees. Quite obviously, you shouldn't pay the auditors $10,000, for example, if you think that your child was underpaid by less than $5,000.

Therefore, the best way to make sure that Audit Rights can actually be used is to include language in the contract that makes clear when the person or organization being audited has to pay for the audit. For example, the contract could provide that the people being audited must pay for the auditors if the audit reveals more than a specified amount of missed payments.

> *In the event that the results of the audit establish that more than $5000 is due to the auditing party, the auditing party shall be entitled to reimbursement of reasonable accountant costs incurred in undertaking the audit.*

Remember, this language would also apply to you. It would give the Talent Agent or Talent Manager the ability to audit your books to make sure, for example, that you reimbursed all of the costs that were due to them. This is a strong incentive for you to keep good and accurate records and to treat your child's career as a business, and not just a hobby.

The best way to make sure that your child is, in fact, being properly paid is to keep track of and closely monitor your child's expenses and income. Audit rights are particularly helpful if your Talent Agent or Talent Manager isn't responding to your requests for receipts, statements, and other financial information. Audit Rights are an important additional source of protection for you and your family.

# Summary of Part IV

## Follow the Money: Understanding Compensation

Hollywood is a business. Your entertainment son or daughter and your family can only be fully protected if you understand how people are paid.

- Talent Agents and Talent Managers are paid on a commission basis. Typically it's a 10% commission for agents and a 15% commission for managers.

- Unless your contract with them specifically excludes a revenue source, these percentages are calculated on all gross revenues, including, potentially, projects that could take place after the contract ends. Make sure you understand what is included or excluded from the commission calculation.

- SAG-AFTRA union contracts establish the minimum amounts that performers earn in most Films, TV series, or TV commercials.

- The performers who earn the most generally have the bargaining power that comes from being sought by name. When the people who pay performers want someone specific to play a particular role, that person has bargaining power to command top dollar.

- SAG-AFTRA union contracts also play a crucial role in providing health insurance and related benefits. Receiving health insurance, for example, depends on earning more than the annual minimum threshold. The current minimums are approximately $15,000 a year for the basic coverage and about $30,000 a year for the higher-level coverage.

- Your Talent Agent and talent management contract should include language specifying how costs will be paid, and which expenses require parental pre-approval.

- Income taxes, Coogan Trust Account distributions, and talent agency commissions are paid before your child is paid.

- Make arrangements with a tax professional to make sure that taxes on your child's income are covered.

- Make sure that your contracts with Talent Agents and managers include mutual audit rights.

Despite what some parents seem to believe, the best way to make money in entertainment is for your child to work hard, get along with others, and work long enough so that he/she can be on a TV show that becomes a hit or obtain significant roles in Motion Pictures. Being a high-maintenance performer usually causes children to have shorter careers and to be paid less rather than more. Think long-term and think big!

# PART V

*Protecting Entertainment Kids From
Paparazzi and Predators*

# PROTECTING ENTERTAINMENT KIDS FROM PAPARAZZI AND PREDATORS

This book would simply not be complete without addressing two important topics that threaten the physical, emotional, and psychological wellbeing of our entertainment industry children. Kids in Hollywood, by virtue of the money they can and do make and their notoriety and visibility, are more of a target than typical children or young adults. The law has and is continuing to recognize this fact. California, in particular, passed laws designed to protect young people who have attained some degree of celebrity or who are pursuing their road to fame.

Part V includes the following chapters:

- Hollywood Children and the Paparazzi
- Protecting Your Family from Sexual Predators

# CHAPTER 28

## HOLLYWOOD CHILDREN AND THE PAPARAZZI

*I believe in equality for everyone, except reporters and paparazzi.*

—Mahatma Gandhi

Paparazzi: "Freelance photographers who aggressively pursue celebrities for the purpose of taking candid photographs." *Merriam-Webster's Collegiate Dictionary*, Eleventh Edition, 2009

Paparazzi: "They converge several times a week like flies on a dead carcass. Blocking the street, the sidewalk, hanging their cameras over the fence. Making boatloads of noise, just for a glimpse of Lindsay Lohan. . . . " Tammara, "The Paparazzi Pursuit," *L.A. METBLOGS* (August 11, 2009)

Even *Merriam-Webster's* neutral and bland definition of paparazzi mentions that they are aggressive. This is, however, too narrow a view. As an advocate and protector of children in entertainment, I know that the paparazzi pose a serious potential threat not only to celebrities and their children, but also to up-and-coming stars of all ages, not to mention children of celebrities and non-celebrity bystanders who might innocently get caught between the paparazzi and their celebrity prey. However, as a lawyer, I am also well aware of our longstanding, but sometimes conflicting, tradition of protecting freedom of speech and of the press.

What motivates paparazzi? In a word—Money! Television media outlets and entertainment publications, whether in print or online, pay extraordinary fees, reportedly often in excess of $100,000 for "the right" photograph. Rumors have it that the final picture of Michael Jackson before his sad and untimely death sold for an incredible $500,000.

"Paparazzi" became a household term in 1997, with the tragic death of Princess Diana. A British jury later found that her death was "caused by the gross negligence of her speeding driver and *pursuing paparazzi*." Princess Diana's death triggered an enormous worldwide back-

## THE ORIGIN OF THE WORD PARAZZI

*The word "paparazzi" first appeared in the 1960 Film "La Dolce Vita," directed by Frederico Fellini. Fellini explained that he coined the term from an Italian word for "sparrow," because the photographers hopping and scurrying around celebrities reminded him of the little birds. As a result he used the Italian word for sparrow (paparazzi) as the name for the photographer, who was a friend of the main character in "La Dolce Vita."*

lash. Lawmakers hurriedly tried to pass laws to prevent a similar tragedy. In the United States, Congress proposed several bills but none became law.

A year after Princess Diana's death, California took the matter into its own hands and our then-Governor, Pete Wilson, signed into law the original California Anti-Paparazzi Act. The Act evolved over time and was first strengthened with a 2005 amendment.

In 2009, then-Governor Arnold Schwarzenegger signed a second amendment to California's Anti-Paparazzi Act, which took effect on January 1, 2010. Actress Jennifer Aniston influenced passage of the new law after the famous *Friends* actress shared horror stories about her encounters with paparazzi with the California Assemblywoman who was behind passage of the amendment.

In passing the 2009 amendment, the California legislature found that *harsher civil penalties* were needed because "legitimate privacy interests of individuals and their families have been violated," and that "individuals and their families have been harassed and endangered by being persistently followed and chased" by the paparazzi.

Most recently, in August 2013, supported by the compelling presence of actresses Halle Berry and Jennifer Garner, the California legislature held what should be considered the most significant and dramatic breakthrough hearings to step up the protections for a targeted group—children of celebrities—by proposing *criminal penalties* against violating paparazzi. The two actresses/parents testified before the Senate about some of the horrors their children and the children of other celebrities must face at the hands of the paparazzi.

In early September 2013, thanks to the efforts of Sen. Kevin de Leon, Berry, Garner and others, what was known as Senate Bill 606, (discussed further below), passed and the final version of the new law was signed by Governor Jerry Brown just three weeks later and become law on January 1, 2014.

You might be wondering why paparazzi simply can't be prohibited outright from following celebrities and their children. Why does the legislature have to find that "legitimate privacy rights are being violated" before it can implement laws to protect people?

The answer is the tug-of-war between the First Amendment's broad protections of *newsworthy speech* on the one hand and a person's *privacy rights* on the other. Throughout history, scholars and judges have defined the right to privacy to mean "the right to be let alone." Although the U.S. Constitution does not explicitly create a right to privacy, courts have found that "zones of privacy" exist, where we can reasonably expect that our privacy will be protected. It is also clear that the right to privacy extends to children as well.

Under California's privacy laws, there are certain private situations and places in which private citizens' photographs cannot be taken. However, defining what is private can be problematic, especially when someone becomes a public figure or celebrity. Once individuals become public figures, their privacy rights are often waived, or at least very limited. That is why lawmakers can only prohibit specific circumstances in which paparazzi may not photograph celebrities.

## WHAT ARE PAPARAZZI PROHIBITED FROM DOING?

Paparazzi violate the 2009 law in California if it can be established that a photograph was taken or was intended to be taken under one of the following circumstances: (1) a physical invasion of privacy, (2) a constructive invasion of privacy, or (3) an assault. Let's look at all three.

### Physical Invasion of Privacy

For a *physical invasion* to take place, one must show that a *trespass* has occurred. A trespass, however, cannot happen if the paparazzi are in a public place. Since many, if not most, encounters with the paparazzi take place in public places, such as retail shopping outlets, airports, and restaurants, it is hard to establish a *physical invasion* of privacy in those places, and, as a result, this protection is very limited.

If three paparazzi approach your child in a public place, such as a public sidewalk on Rodeo Drive in Beverly Hills, it is virtually impossible to claim an expectation of privacy in that setting. However, one area in which children and families may be protected by the *physical invasion* rule is if the paparazzi do trespass on property, such as jumping fences to take the picture.

### Constructive Invasion of Privacy

What is a constructive invasion of privacy and how does it work? This is intended to limit the situation where the paparazzi use telephoto lenses or other advanced technology to capture close-up images and video from a distance, without the person being aware that it is happening, and when the person has a reasonable expectation of privacy. The classic situation is when photographs are taken of someone sunbathing on the roof of her private estate, or sharing a private moment in a private hotel bungalow with a friend or guest. Capturing such photographs constitutes constructive invasion of privacy, because without the use of the advanced technology, the photographs would not be possible, and the person photographed likely had a reasonable expectation of privacy in that moment.

### Assault by the Paparazzi

Photographs taken during an assault most obviously violate the 2009 law. An assault covers a wide range of activity, but the essence is the use or threat of force that causes fear of offensive or harmful contact. Thus, while paparazzi may stand on the sidewalk and take a picture of a young star walking down a public street, they may not use force, or threaten to use force, to capture that image. They don't have to actually touch the person to commit assault; it's enough that they cause a reasonable fear of imminent harm or of an offensive touching.

### If the Paparazzi Illegally Take a Picture of Your Child

The 2009 amendment to the Anti-Paparazzi Act substantially expanded the liability, of the individual paparazzo who photographs a celebrity if it can be shown that he or she had "actual knowledge" that the photo was taken illegally. It appears that the law was designed to remove the paparazzi's financial incentive to use illegal means to take pictures of celebrities. The 2009 law does this by imposing a civil fine of not less than $5,000 and not more than $50,000 on paparazzi, agents of the paparazzi, and on the first person involved in the sale or offer for sale of any visual image, if the person has "actual knowledge" that the image was taken in violation of the statute. These fines are in addition to the potential for substantial money damages that prior versions of the law imposed on paparazzi.

### PROTECTING THE MOST VULNERABLE— THE CHILDREN OF CELEBRITIES

The new law, effective January 1, 2014, amended *Penal Code* Section 11414 relating to harassment, in the context of protecting children of celebrities from paparazzi. Unlike the 2009 Anti-Paparazzi Act, which are civil law, the new laws are criminally based and provide that any person who intentionally harasses the child of any other person because of that person's employment (e.g., actor, actress, musician, etc.) shall be punished by imprisonment in a county jail for a term not exceeding one year, or by a fine not exceeding $10,000, or by both the fine and imprisonment.

Harassment, under the new law, means "knowing and willful conduct directed at a specific child" that "seriously alarms, annoys, torments or terrorizes the child" and that serves no legitimate purpose and that takes place "during the course of any actual or attempted recording of the child's image or voice" without the express consent of the parent, when "following the child's activities or by lying in wait."

A second harrassment conviction shall be punished by a fine not exceeding $20,000 and by imprisonment in a county jail for not less than five days but not exceeding one year, and a third (or subsequent) conviction shall be punished by a fine not exceeding $30,000 and by imprisonment in a county jail for not less than thirty days but not exceeding one year.

Additionally, upon a violation of the new law, the parent may bring a civil action against the violating paparazzi on behalf of the child, and seek remedies for actual damages, punitive damages, attorney's fees, costs, and disgorgement of any compensation from the sale or license of the child's image received by the individual paparazzo and anyone who violated the law.

## WHAT ELSE CAN BE DONE?

Our celebrity-obsessed culture has, in recent years, evolved to include a never-before-seen thirst for photographs, video clips or any image of the children of celebrities. That hunger continues to grow. Many of us remember all the fuss that was made when the first pictures of Suri Cruise (daughter of Tom Cruise and Katie Holmes) hit the entertainment news. In fact, the births of celebrity children are now often the top stories on entertainment TV, and are instantly sprawled across the cover pages of entertainment magazines, tabloids and Internet websites on a daily basis. And the reason we have access to these images is very simple—the paparazzi!

Is the combination of the 2009 *civil laws* and the 2014 *criminal laws* enough to deter paparazzi from taking illegal steps to photograph celebrities and their children? Given the huge amounts that some publications and websites are willing to pay for photos, only time will really tell if, and to what extent, paparazzi abuses will continue.

One of the simplest and most effective potential remedies would seem to be implementing "buffer zones" in family and child-orientated locations, such as schools, parks and medical facilities. This is one of the excellent suggestions made by Lauren N. Follett, a lawyer who recently graduated from the University of Southern California Gould School of Law. A proposed "Buffer Zone" law was introduced by Assembly Member Richard Bloom of Santa Monica, California, in February, 2013, as AB 1256, but unfortunately it never made its way out of the State Assembly for a vote in the State Senate.

However, Ms. Follett's article on the subject, entitled "Taming the Paparazzi in the Wild West," is compelling, so let's take a look at her arguments for Buffer Zones, as most of the following is taken from her fascinating discussion on the subject.

Several things lead to the belief that buffer zones would be effective. As Ms. Follet notes, the City of Santa Monica, where many celebrities and their families live, held City Council hearings regarding the implementation of buffer zones around Santa Monica medical facilities, hospitals, and schools. Among the pieces of evidence introduced during the hearings is a rather graphic video that shows just how severe the paparazzi problem can be. The video was taken at the First Presbyterian Nursery School (attended by Meg Ryan's son and by the young daughter of Jennifer Garner and Ben Affleck). The video, which is posted on the Paparazzi Reform Initiatives website (www.paparazzi-reform.org), shows that the paparazzi had "created a dangerous, circus-like environment not only for the celebrities and their pupil children, but also for other parents and their children who attend the school." Furthermore, according to Ms. Follet, parents complained "of feeling trapped, being verbally and physically assaulted, having their children nearly trampled by the paparazzi and seeing paparazzi climb up a fence to take pictures of celebrity children on the playground."

Buffer zones would not prohibit paparazzi from being present; they would still have an opportunity to take photographs at a distance. It would, however, prevent them from creating an environment that posed a threat to the safety of other children, parents, and bystanders.

The buffer zone concept is also likely to be legal. As Ms. Follet correctly notes, the U.S. Supreme Court decided that "fixed buffer zones" (i.e., those which surround a stationary or permanent location) can be constitutional. As with many constitutional issues, the legality of buffer zones to protect children from paparazzi depends on how judges evaluate the competing interests of safety and freedom of the press. There is reason to think that, in the case of paparazzi who take pictures of children, the judges might conclude that the law favors the children. Here is how Ms. Follet summarizes the issue:

> *[I]n the case of paparazzi and photographing celebrity children, the government interest in keeping schools, parks and medical facilities safe for families and children seems to outweigh the interest in freedom of the press and free speech. . . [T]he government has an interest in maintaining public safety and order by ensuring that parents and their children (regardless of notoriety) are kept out of harm's way while they are at these important, family-orientated locations—walking their children through school parking lots to their classrooms, helping them down slides at the park, or taking them to medical appointments.*

We should be grateful that our lawmakers and government representatives have initiated both civil and now criminal anti-paparazzi laws, and continue to review and amend those laws to address current and modern-day concerns to protect children of celebrities and celebrity children.

I also admire people like Jennifer Aniston, Halle Berry, Jennifer Garner, and Lauren Follett for offering and being part of forward-looking solutions for dealing with this problem and hope to see a revised version of AB 1256 introduced in the future. Working together, we can and must continue to take action to prevent Princess Diana-type tragedies from striking again—and particularly from harming all of our entertainment children.

# CHAPTER 29

## PROTECTING YOUR FAMILY FROM SEXUAL PREDATORS

*Cruelty might be very human, and it might be cultural,*
*but it's not acceptable.*

—Jodie Foster in her
Academy Awards Acceptance Speech, 1989

This is a difficult topic, but entertainment kids are subject to different risk factors and circumstances that make them particularly good targets of sexual predators, so we must address it. Child molestation, sexual abuse, and pedophilia are not new problems and are not particular to Hollywood or entertainment kids. In fact, the chances of your up-and-coming child star experiencing such a life-changing nightmare are miniscule. Becoming an educated parent will reduce those risks even further.

This chapter will not only briefly discuss child molesters in Hollywood, but also how sexual predators position themselves to initiate and carry out abuse against children, ways that parents can protect their own children from these predators, and how California lawmakers are now aggressively addressing the problem.

### ENTERTAINMENT INDUSTRY PREDATORS IN THE NEWS

In a January 8, 2012 article, *Los Angeles Times* writer Dawn C. Chmielewski reported that "[at] least a dozen child molestation and child photography prosecutions since 2000 have involved actors, managers, production assistants and others in the entertainment industry." Her impressive article outlines several of the more prominent, albeit disturbing, cases of abuse.

One case involved child abuse, criminal charges, a conviction, and a six-year sentence against a production assistant who was working for Nickelodeon—one of the nation's most well-known producers of children's television programming. Another involved a registered sex offender working as a temporary production assistant, this time at Nickelodeon's Animation Studio. He was convicted in 2009 and sentenced to six months in jail. But the conviction, a felony, was thrown out on appeal. Since then, Nickelodeon has clearly and publicly stated that it has toughened its employment screening, which now includes full background checks on anyone who works for Nickelodeon— and this includes the parents of child actors.

While many reported sexual predators are themselves young adults, two of the more recent Hollywood scandals involve, in unrelated events, fifty-nine-year-old Grammy- and Emmy-winning composer Fernando Rivas and Hollywood children's Talent Manager, Marty Weiss, age 47. Rivas, who worked as a *Sesame Street* employee and a music composer for both Disney and Nickelodeon, was first arrested earlier in 2011. He was finally charged in a South Carolina Federal Court on November 21, 2011, for allegedly producing child pornography and coercing a child to engage in sexually explicit conduct.

Only days later, on November 29, 2011, Weiss was arrested in Los Angeles for allegedly repeatedly abusing a boy who sought his career guidance. Weiss was initially charged and pled not guilty to eight felony counts, alleging sodomy and lewd acts with a minor, and was held in the Los Angeles County Jail on $800,000 bail as he awaited further hearings. Six months later, during a pre-trial hearing, he pled "no contest" (i.e., while not admitting guilt, he did not dispute the charges against him) to two charges of oral copulation with a child under the age of fourteen. He was sentenced to one year in jail and five years' probation. The sentence was suspended for time already served (six months), and he was released at that time. Weiss was ordered to register as a sex offender and enter a treatment program, and it was reported that he is not permitted to be in the presence of anyone under eighteen years of age without another adult present. Many people were appalled and outraged by the lenient sentence. Others felt the case against him was weak, if not exaggerated. I was acquainted with Marty Weiss, and his arrest and conviction not only sickened me personally, but certainly reignited, as it should, the long-standing debate in the TV and motion picture industry regarding children's safety.

In a riveting and timely interview in August 2011, shortly *before* either Fernando Rivas or Marty Weiss were charged, former child star Corey Feldman told ABC's *Nightline* "there's a lot of good people in this industry but there's also a lot of really, really sick corrupt people in this industry...and...the number one problem in Hollywood was, and is and always will be, pedophilia" which, he adds, is always done "under the radar." He also avowed that, as he grew from an infant actor to child stardom through classic 1980s Films like *Gremlins, The Goonies, The Lost Boys*, and of course, *Stand By Me*, he was "surrounded" by pedophiles operating "like vultures."

So why does this happen? What are the telltale signs? And, what can you do to protect your child?

## How to Identify Sexual Predators

**ROBERT'S WARNINGS:** Sexual molestation experts uniformly describe a process known as "Grooming Children for Sexual Molestation" or just "Grooming," which increases the predator's access to the victim and decreases the likelihood of being caught. According to the State of California Department of Justice, in the majority of child abuse cases, perpetrators gain access to their victims through coercion, seldom using physical force. Furthermore, once the abuse has taken place, children often do not tell of the abuse for a variety of reasons, including fear of harm towards their loved ones, shame, and the fear of losing the offender, who may be very important to the child and the child's family.

In his book *Child Molesters: A Behavioral Analysis*, Kenneth Lanning, a former FBI agent, identifies five stages of the grooming process, each smoothly transitioning to the next until the sexual predator abuses his young victim. A summary of Lanning's five stages, as applicable to the entertainment industry, is as follows:

1. Victim selection and identification: While every child is vulnerable to abuse, molesters have a specific preference, and while some choose young girls and others might choose young boys, one of the most common traits a sexual predator looks for is the most obvious weakness of the victim. Observant parents should be looking for people who have a special bond or special relationship with your child, as this makes the predator's job of identifying and exploiting his or her weakness much easier. Child molesters are particularly drawn to the entertainment industry because of the opportu-

nities to take advantage of the hopes, dreams, and aspirations of young actors and models. Children, and often parents of children, want the fame and fortune that the industry offers, and this becomes the very enticement that a pedophile can use against his victims.

2.  Background information and checking: The shrewd sexual predator does not seek information by asking parents or other people who might become suspicious and report back to a parent, but rather gains information about a child's needs, wants, dreams, and desires from simple and regular ongoing conversations that extract this information directly from your child over time.

3.  Filling a need: Child molesters are very skilled at being available, and at fulfilling the needs and desires of your child. This can be done through giving simple gifts, treating your child to food, or taking him/her to special industry events, all of which lures the child by providing him or her with attention, and by fulfilling his/her needs and wants, and keeping his/her dreams squarely in front of him/her. This, at the same time, puts the child molester in the position of filling these needs and desires, or in a position to teach, coach, and promise success about aspects of the business important to your child.

4.  Lowering and decreasing inhibitions: The grooming process starts moving along more quickly when the sexual predator has developed enough trust to lower your child's inhibitions regarding sexual issues. This can be done by subtly coercing a child to watch sexually explicit material and convincing him or her that sex is normal and casual, rather than sacred.

5.  Abuse initiation: The grooming process is complete when the initial sexual abuse begins. Research shows that the first physical touching between a child molester and the child is usually non-sexual, as it is designed to test limits, break down inhibitions, and desensitize the child. That, of course, leads to the ultimate and eventual sexual contact and abuse, with traumatic consequences that can even cause long-term or permanent emotional disorders.

News reports and other commentary regarding the Marty Weiss

scandal suggest that, before his arrest, Weiss was overly social, had sleepovers and went on road trips with underage clients—without their parents. If these reports are true, and whether or not this behavior ultimately led to other inappropriate relations, every parent needs to understand that this is *not* normal or acceptable conduct between a Talent Manager and an underage actor. This type of behavior, given what we just learned about grooming, should now be a red flag for any parent.

While an exhaustive discussion of the subject of grooming is beyond the scope of this book, parents and guardians of children in entertainment who become aware of the grooming process are in a better position to more easily recognize and prevent impending harm. The bottom line is that parents and guardians simply have to face the reality that every child is susceptible, and entertainment kids are at high risk due to the lure of fame and fortune and the adult environment of the industry. Understanding the grooming process and making sure you have a strong and healthy bond with your child, coupled with open communication and trust, will help tremendously in protecting your child *before* he or she suffers at the hands of a child molester.

If you discover or suspect that your child has been the victim of a child molester or sexual predator, please be sure to immediately contact an experienced mental health professional and sexual abuse lawyer for guidance and counsel on exactly how best to proceed.

## CALIFORNIA'S NEW CHILD PERFORMER'S PROTECTION ACT

In an attempt to attack this problem head-on, California Assemblywoman Nora Campos, of San Jose, who sits on the Committee on Arts, Entertainment, Sports, Tourism and Internet Media, introduced a proposed new law, (AB 1660, which became *Labor Code* §1706, et seq. on January 1, 2013), which is known as the Child Performer's Services Permits Act. The Act, which California Governor Jerry Brown signed into law in September 2012, requires currently *unregulated* entertainment professionals to submit an application to the California Labor Commissioner, pay a small fee, and undergo fingerprinting and a criminal background check conducted by the FBI. If the background check comes back clean, the California Labor Commissioner will issue a Child Performer's Services Permit, which will have to be renewed every two years.

Currently *unregulated* entertainment professionals would include, among others, Talent Managers, entertainment career counselors, photographers, acting and voice coaches, dance teachers, and publicists who work with children under the age of eighteen. Since Talent Agents *are already licensed* and studio teachers already *undergo rigorous scrutiny* they, and a few others, would not be required to hold a permit.

The new law hopes to help fill an existing loophole, by requiring a permit for the unregulated, and is designed to prevent sexual predators from victimizing the unsuspecting and uninformed. It also *prohibits those who are registered sex offenders from providing services to young Hollywood.* And any person who willfully violates any provision of the Child Performer's Services Permits Act is guilty of criminal misdemeanor and each violation is punishable by a fine "not exceeding ten thousand dollars ($10,000), by imprisonment in a county jail for not more than one year, or both that fine and imprisonment."

To help you, as a parent, keep informed, the Labor Commissioner launched on October 11, 2013 an online website where entertainment professionals can apply for the permit *and* where parents can search for *permit holders.* Go to: www.permits.dir.ca.gov/cps/index.jsp.

I was proud to have actively participated in passage of this new law by testifying in support before both the California Assembly and Senate. It is a good law, and it provides additional important protections for children in the entertainment industry and their parents.

## What You as a Parent Can Do

When it comes to protecting your child from Hollywood child molesters and sexual abusers, remember three things:

First, while implementing new laws is very important, nothing will protect your child better than good parenting and having smart and educated kids. Simply stated, we cannot delegate parental responsibilities to legislators, the police, the District Attorney, or a big production company. Talk to your children. Teach them to be alert and wary of any physical contact by an adult and to come to you with their problems.

As Paul Petersen explains, "family education is the key ingredient to a productive future." Paul is a former child star, and President of "A Minor Consideration," a non-profit, tax-deductible foundation formed to give guidance and support to young performers. Heed Paul's advice. Visit his website: www.minorcon.org.

Secondly, the days are gone when it is enough to just tell your child to "stay away from strangers." This was especially true when it comes to teaching about child molesters. The fact is, the majority of children are molested by those they know and trust, and on most TV, Film, and commercial shoots, young performers will likely come in contact with talented professionals whom they don't know.

Thirdly, we can warn our children of potential danger and help them understand the proper boundaries for adults *without alarming or frightening them.* It's all in how you, as a parent, approach the subject and talk with your child. When my children were younger, I learned that it was best to first explain that most adults are concerned about their protection and want them to achieve their goals and dreams, but that there are some people who are not, and even a few who might be willing to take advantage of them or hurt them. Just as teaching my two children to avoid putting their hand on a hot stove did not instill a fear of cooking, teaching how child abusers groom their victims won't create a generation of paranoid children, stifle the joys and rewards of acting and modeling, or raise unwarranted suspicion regarding the vast majority of children's Talent Agents, Talent Managers, acting coaches, producers, and directors, who are truly dedicated. Rather, it will educate and inform, so that you and your child are positioned for, as Paul Petersen says, "a productive future" and a safer environment in which to fulfill your child's dreams and goals.

# Summary of Part V

## Protecting Entertainment Children
## From Paparazzi and Predators

Children in the entertainment industry face certain risks that most youngsters do not. Specifically, young stars and their families might need to protect themselves from abusive paparazzi. In addition, entertainment children are more likely than the average child to be targeted by sexual predators. These risks are very small, but there are certain steps parents can take to reduce these risks even further.

### With Respect to Paparazzi

- Under California law, paparazzi and the people who knowingly sell illegal pictures taken by paparazzi can face heavy fines.

- Paparazzi may take pictures of young stars when they appear in public places or other locations, such as public sidewalks, where we don't have a reasonable expectation of privacy.

- Paparazzi may not, however, trespass on property or commit assaults when they take pictures of celebrities or their children.

- California has, for fifteen years, expanded legal protections relating to paparazzi. Parents of entertainment kids can play an important role in advocating the establishment of "buffer zones," and taking other steps that will further protect our entertainment kids.

### With Respect to Sexual Predators

- Understand that sexual predators don't act randomly. Experts have identified a five-step grooming process that sexual predators use to identify and carry out sexual assaults on their victims.

- While Talent Managers, Talent Agents and others who represent children often get to know their clients very well, it is not normal or typical for them to host unsupervised sleepovers or get overly social with your children. As with any adult, this kind of conduct should raise red flags.

- The best defense against predators is to maintain good parental relations with your children. Know where they are, communicate with them often, and don't let others take over your role.

The risks associated with paparazzi, and especially predators, are worth exploring in detail because they can lead to dreadful, yet avoidable consequences.

To protect your child, however, you also need to know what to do when business relationships with Talent Agents and Talent Managers end in more routine ways. Part VI discusses how best to end the working relationship with a Talent Agent or manager and what to do when the agent or Talent Manager wants to terminate his contract with you.

# PART VI

*Getting Out of Entertainment Contracts*

# PART VI

## GETTING OUT OF ENTERTAINMENT CONTRACTS

Entertainment is a relationship-oriented business. That's why this book has gone into so much detail explaining the respective roles of Talent Agents, Talent Managers, and other industry insiders with whom you and your child will interact.

While we have focused on how to make these relationships work, unfortunately, that won't always happen. Some relationships last longer than others. In other words, the more involved you and your child become, the more likely it is that at some point in time, a talent agency, talent management or public relations relationship will end. In the course of your child's career, you may think about getting out of a relationship, or someone will let you know that he is no longer interested in representing your child.

Part VI describes various ways in which entertainment contracts can be ended, and includes the following chapters:

- Craig and MeShiel End Their Talent Management Contract

- Terminating Entertainment Contracts: The Basics

- Changing Representation: Talent Agents, Talent Managers, and Entertainment Attorneys

- A Child's Right to Disaffirm (Cancel) a Contract

- Preventing Disaffirmance by Seeking Court Approval

- "Insurance" Against Disaffirmance: Seeking Parental Agreement

# CHAPTER 30

## CRAIG AND MeSHIEL END THEIR
## TALENT MANAGEMENT CONTRACT

*I have a sense of destiny that you are led to
things you are supposed to do.*

—Robert Downey, Jr.

There was, for quite some time, a productive relationship between Talent Manager Sharyn Berg, on the one hand, and Craig Traylor and his mother MeShiel, on the other. MeShiel signed a three-year contract with Sharyn in January 1999. A year later, Craig booked and appeared in the TV Pilot for *Malcolm in the Middle*. Initially, his character, Stevie Kenarbin, was supposed to be a minor character. But Craig did such a good job, and the show became increasingly popular, so Craig's recurring role on the show was virtually on par with, and ultimately evolved into, a Series Regular role.

During its first season (January-May 2000), Craig appeared in 11 of the 16 episodes that aired. The following season (November 2000-May 2001), Craig appeared in an additional thirteen episodes.

*Malcolm in the Middle* established itself in its first two seasons as both a ratings hit and a critical success. The show's director, Todd Holland, won the Emmy for Best Director in a Comedy Series in both 2000 and 2001. Likewise, the show's writers won an Emmy for their work during the second season, and Executive Producer Linwood Bloomer was nominated for an Emmy for Best Original comedy series. Three Series Regulars, Frankie Muniz (playing Malcolm), Jane Kaczmarek (playing Lois), and Bryan Cranston (playing Hal), were nominated for Emmys and/or Golden Globes for their performances.

Craig Traylor also received recognition for his work. In 2000, he won the Young Artist Award, Best Ensemble in a TV Series (Comedy or Drama), and the Young Artist Award, Best Performance in a TV Comedy Series - Supporting Young Actor. He was also nominated for the Image Award, Outstanding Youth Actor/Actress, the Young Artist Award, Best Performance in a TV Comedy Series—Supporting Young Actor, and the Young Artist Award, Best Ensemble in a TV Series

(Drama or Comedy).

But as we know, not all good things will always last forever. Unfortunately, personal problems began to surface for the Traylor family during this time. In addition, MeShiel's financial advisor informed her that to resolve certain financial issues she must reduce expenses, which caused her to contemplate whether Craig really needed ongoing representation by Sharyn Berg, Craig's talent manger.

Thus, on September 11, 2001—yes, that 9/11—MeShiel wrote Sharyn Berg a letter. This was approximately four months before their Talent Management Agreement was scheduled to expire. In the letter, MeShiel outlined her financial concerns and informed Sharyn Berg that she was terminating their relationship. MeShiel acknowledged that she owed Sharyn money and promised that it would be paid. As a courtesy and token of appreciation to Sharyn, MeShiel also voluntarily waived the right to a 5% commission against the earnings of twins she had referred to Sharyn. MeShiel also pointed out that, since Craig had not gotten any new auditions or new work in recent months, she simply had to terminate the contract.

Although MeShiel could not have foreseen it at the time, the letter she wrote to Sharyn Berg unleashed a series of events that would not be resolved *for more than five years*. As the next chapters make clear, ending a formal business relationship in the entertainment industry, including one with a Talent Manager or Talent Agent, involves critical issues for parents and their entertainment children. There is often much more to it than just writing a letter.

> **ROBERT'S TIPS:** Different sets of rules apply to ending different kinds of entertainment contracts. Ending a contract with a Talent Manager may, depending on certain factors, be different than from terminating a Talent Agent agreement. And contracts with studios and production companies fall into a separate category.

Before explaining the differences in terminating these specific kinds of contracts, it's essential that you, as a parent, understand the basics of terminating an entertainment contract. Let's cover that next.

# CHAPTER 31

## TERMINATING ENTERTAINMENT CONTRACTS: THE BASICS

*Everything has to come to an end, sometime.*

—L. Frank Baum
*The Marvelous Land of Oz*

There are three basic ways that an entertainment industry contract can be terminated. One involves mutual consent. A second relates to the timing of the contract. A third comes into play when people who enter into a contract don't live up to the promises they made in the contract. Let's look at these in turn.

## TERMINATING A CONTRACT BY MUTUAL CONSENT

Contracts with Talent Agents and Talent Managers frequently end by way of a mutual understanding and agreement. This happens when you and your child's Talent Agent or manager agree to go your separate ways. This can happen, for example, because for one reason or another, you *feel* your child isn't (or he or she actually isn't) getting enough auditions or a personality conflict develops between you and your child and his or her representative. Alternatively, after a reasonable time has passed, and the Talent Manager or Talent Agent has secured no commissions from working with your child, or your child has not booked any projects, either you or your child's Talent Agent or Talent Manager may conclude that "this isn't working." Once Talent Agents and Talent Managers begin to earn money working with your child, they are substantially less likely to want to end your contract before it expires.

The law refers to this situation as termination by mutual consent, but that doesn't necessarily mean that everyone is equally happy about the end of the relationship. Sometimes the Talent Agent or Talent Manager initiates the break-up because they have concluded that they would prefer to spend time working with someone else who appears more likely to be successful and thus generate commissions. Sometimes actors or their parents initiate the split, because they lose confidence in the Talent Agent or Talent Manager, or are disappointed by the results of working with him. In these circumstances, it is natural for the side that initiated the end of the relationship to feel better about the situation. But, as long as both sides ultimately agree to stop working together, this is considered a termination by mutual consent.

## TERMINATING A CONTRACT: TIMING ISSUES

A second, straightforward way to end an entertainment contract is to wait for it to expire. Thus, a three-year contract ends three years from the date it was signed, or on the date indicated in the contract itself. This is the easiest way to terminate a contract, because you don't have to do anything other than wait for the contract period to end.

Many entertainment contracts, however, include provisions that require you to do something to terminate them. As discussed in Chapter 15, for example, contracts with Talent Managers may include automatic renewals. In contracts with such provisions, if you do nothing, the contract automatically continues for one, two, three, or more years.

When your contract includes an automatic extension provision or any other language that requires you to do something to terminate the contract, follow the instructions in the contract as precisely as you can. For example, if the contract says that you need to send a first-class letter postmarked no later than September 30 to a particular address, do exactly that. Don't rely on a telephone call or email. Follow the notification requirements—precisely.

This level of precision also applies to opt-out clauses. As discussed in Chapter 16, an opt-out clause can give you and your child additional protections when dealing with Talent Managers. In California, the standard Talent Agent contract includes an opt-out clause that allows you and your child to get out of the contact before the full contract term. But many contracts with Talent Managers don't include an opt-out clause unless you negotiate for one to be included in the contract. So, for example, if your opt-out clause provides that you can get out of the contract after a period without a booking, follow that deadline as precisely as you can. Do your best not to miss the deadline, and again, follow the notification requirements precisely.

### *What if You Miss a Deadline?*
Continuing with the example described above, what happens if you mail a letter terminating the contract on October 1, instead of September 30, as required by the contract? Or perhaps you notify your Talent

Manager verbally that you will opt out of the contract on September 15, but you don't get around to sending a letter until October 15. Does missing these deadlines mean that you have lost the right to opt out of the contract, or that the contract will automatically continue (under the automatic extension provision)?

It depends. This is, admittedly, an unsatisfying answer. If it were possible to provide a comprehensive answer, I would. But the clearest piece of advice you can get is to talk to an experienced entertainment lawyer. The basic laws of contracts have existed for hundreds of years. Over that time, numerous exceptions have been recognized. Sometimes missing a deadline, by even a day, means that you lose the right to opt out of an agreement. But sometimes the deadline isn't interpreted so narrowly. You may have some wiggle room, which is why you should talk to a lawyer even if you are convinced that you missed the deadline.

## TERMINATING THE CONTRACT: CONDUCT ISSUES

A contract can also be terminated if the other side doesn't fulfill the promises it has made in the contract. The technical term for this is "breaching the contract." If you break or breach the contract, the contract can often be terminated.

But this isn't an automatic termination. If you feel that the other side hasn't lived up to its obligation, you can often take steps to end the contract (regardless of the timing issues involved). Thus, if a Talent Manager doesn't fulfill a responsibility, for example, to advise and counsel you in your career, or to secure a Talent Agent for you (if this was promised), that could be a valid reason to end the contract.

This rule also applies to you. If you or your child do not fulfill your obligations under the contract, the other side can move to terminate the contract on that basis. For example, a studio could seek to terminate a performer's contract if an actor or actress repeatedly shows up to the set late, is unprepared, is disruptive on the set, or commits a crime on or off the set. We have seen examples of this in the tabloids and the press over the years.

Generally speaking, only significant breaches of a contract can lead to its termination. The legal term for this is that the breach of contract must be *material*. So, for example, if your child, on one occasion, shows up ten minutes late to the set, that's not going to be a material breach or significant violation of the contract. Likewise, if your Talent

## Case Study

*I have represented and currently represent many high-profile, award-winning and star actors and actresses who have been terribly and very legitimately dissatisfied with the representation of their talent agencies or Talent Managers, for failing to fulfill the written or oral promises made when representation began and everyone was excited about the promises for the future. By the time the problems in the relationship escalate to the point where I receive a call, the complaints are typically serious, but also vary widely—from insufficient auditions, to poorly selecting submission choices, to a lack of bookings, to lack of personal attention, to never truly understanding age ranges or acting role abilities of the actor or actress, to poor attention or ability in negotiating contract rates and other key terms, and sometimes even the ultimate, which means not paying the actor or actress his or her earnings in a timely way, or at all! Depending on the severity and number of complaints, this conduct can and has constituted a breach of contract and become grounds for termination of a talent agency or talent management contract.*

Manager sends your child his/her check a couple of days late, that's also unlikely to be a material breach.

You should be very careful and very thoughtful before accusing someone else of breaching his obligations under an entertainment contract. This can be counterproductive, and may only lead the other side (whether it is a studio, production company, Talent Agent, or Talent Manager) to be even less cooperative, in moving forward. Making this accusation also risks that you and your child will be viewed as being difficult or high-maintenance. And that perception can harm your child's career and be difficult to reverse.

You should, therefore, confer with an experienced entertainment lawyer when you or your child have been accused of not living up to your contractual obligations, or when you feel that your Talent Manager or Talent Agent (or studio or production company) may have materially breached their contractual obligations to you. A lawyer will help you evaluate the potential costs and benefits of various courses of action, ranging from finding ways to get along to taking drastic steps, such as filing a lawsuit. These kinds of discussions are fact-specific. There is no one-size-fits-all approach. That's why it's so important to seek counsel from someone who can help you and your child reach the best decision.

As is explained in detail in the next chapter, most business relationships with Talent Agents, Talent Managers, and entertainment attorneys end by mutual consent.

# CHAPTER 32

## CHANGING REPRESENTATION:
## TALENT AGENTS, TALENT MANAGERS,
## AND ENTERTAINMENT ATTORNEYS

*If you don't like something, change it.*
*If you can't change it, change your attitude.*

—Maya Angelou

There are many reasons why people choose to change or switch Talent Agents or Talent Managers—some very sound and legitimate, others not so much. In fact, during any given week in Hollywood, and particularly following traditional earmarked Seasons (e.g., Pilot Season), both changes and defections from talent agencies and Talent Managers seem to be commonplace. Some argue that the proliferation is a result of the fact that nowadays actors and actresses are more "tuned in" and educated as to what's taking place in Hollywood, which is coupled with the dramatic evolution in television, commercials, and Film production (i.e., less scripted television and more reality television) and the rapid advancements in technology and access to information—a combination which results in "upgrading" and changing representation. Those who view the more rapid turnover in representation less charitably tend to argue that society has become more impatient, less loyal, and unwilling to honor the hard work and effort of those who first took a chance on their child and brought him or her along in the business.

Whatever reason you may have for leaving your Talent Agent or Talent Manager, one thing is generally certain—it is rarely, if ever, an easy task emotionally, and sometimes the emotional difficulty is complicated by the potential legal complications associated with changing representation.

Consider these practical and legal points when changing representation: first, talk with someone you trust and can confide in who will help you honestly and objectively assess whether the potential change of representation is wise or is being made in haste.

Pull out the contract and review all of the provisions that relate to termination. Be sure to read the provision related to the term or length of the contract, as well as any provision related to what happens upon termination. If the contract has an opt-out clause, be clear about what it says.

When a party to a contract follows the opt-out language in the contract, they are exercising a right they have under the contact. By contrast, when someone terminates a contractual relationship, it is more likely that he will be accused of breaking the contract—called "breaching the contract." That is why, in general, fewer legal issues are raised by ending a contract by invoking an opt-out clause than by terminating the contract for other reasons.

If you are less than 100% certain that you understand all of the provisions of the contract and the ramifications related to termination, schedule a one-hour consultation with an entertainment attorney and get clarity. The time and money spent may end up helping you and your family avoid a contentious and expensive lawsuit that could last months or even years.

Before making your final decision, also consider the following issues:

- Are you making this decision because several actor friends are doing so and it seems like a good idea, or is the decision clearly necessary and in your child's best interest?

- Is it possible that a sit-down meeting with your Talent Agent or Talent Manager, in which you openly communicate your concerns, and hopefully get some good answers, might put things right back on track?

- Is the issue more serious? For example, is your child having difficulty getting paid? If so, have you verified that the production has paid your Talent Agent or Talent Manager, in which case an immediate change might be in order?

- Is the impetus for the change a belief that other children seem to be getting more auditions, while you've noticed a lull in auditions for your child? If so, have you truly evaluated whether this is a temporary casting focus on a particular "type" of child who is outside of your child's age, look, or character, or is this something more personal?

- If you are considering leaving because "things have been slow," are you considering the time of year? Is it Pilot Season when the industry is bustling, or is it the summer, when things are often slower for most performers?

- Have you carefully considered whether a new Talent Agent or Talent Manager will be an upgrade over your child's current representation?

- Have you done your homework and researched any new Talent Agent or Talent Manager who might be soliciting you to make sure your child is likely a good match for the new representative, and have you verified that the new talent agency is licensed or that the Talent Manager is legitimate and respected among peers and other talent?

## IF YOU DECIDE TO FIRE YOUR CURRENT TALENT AGENT OR MANAGEMENT REPRESENTATION

There are two critical issues that come into play when deciding to end a relationship with a Talent Agent or Talent Manager. One involves exercising good people skills; the other involves carefully following certain legal formalities.

> **ROBERT'S TIPS:** One of the most important pieces of advice that can be given when terminating a contract—regardless of the reason—is this: Do so with as much integrity, professionalism, and poise as possible. Talent Agents, Talent Managers, parents of child actors, acting coaches, casting directors, producers, directors, and all people in the industry talk among themselves regularly, so avoid all gossip and negative conversation about others in the business, even while terminating a contract.

Experienced Talent Agents and Talent Managers are accustomed to changes in representation, and they know that sometimes it can be the right thing to do. The manner in which you handle the end of the representation can strongly influence how acrimonious the process is and even to what extent Talent Agents and Talent Managers decide to exercise their legal rights under their respective contracts. My experience has shown that when people decide to file a lawsuit or exercise other legal rights, it isn't always because of what the law allows them to do. Oftentimes people are more likely to act aggressively against those who they believe haven't treated them fairly. This is true of everyone. So be sure to take the high road and avoid burning bridges as you make transitions and changes for your child and your family.

You can also protect yourself and your child by making sure that some written evidence exists that makes clear the date on which the representation with the Talent Agent or manager ended. In some circumstances it might also be appropriate to include a brief written description of why the relationship ended. Creating this written note may seem like an unnecessary act, but it can help you avoid future problems.

As suggested above, a decision to terminate a working relationship in the entertainment business often has legal consequences. You will avoid many legal issues and spend a lot less on legal fees if you consult with an experienced entertainment lawyer *before* you decide to end representation with a Talent Agent or Talent Manager.

## TERMINATING YOUR CHILD'S ATTORNEY

As with any professional you hire, there may come a time when you want to fire your entertainment attorney. You may feel, for instance, that your attorney is not acting in your child's best interest and that you might have a better outcome if you were working with a different attorney. Generally speaking, if you are represented by an entertainment lawyer and are unhappy with him or her and feel a change is needed, you have the absolute right, subject to certain special rules, to terminate that relationship at any time.

Those special rules are beyond the scope of this book and also vary from state to state and depend on where the lawyer is licensed to practice. In most states, clients have a wide-ranging ability to fire their lawyer. Before taking that action, I recommend two things. First, review the Attorney-Client Retainer Agreement related to the issue of termination, and second, seriously consider talking to another lawyer before you make any final decisions.

When terminating your attorney, keep in mind that if an attorney is representing your child in a transactional matter (e.g., negotiation of a television or movie contract), terminating and replacing him or her tends to be less complicated than the situation in which the attorney is representing your child in a litigation matter (e.g., a lawsuit by or against a person or studio). This is because some courts will not allow a client to fire an attorney close to the beginning of trial, absent extraordinary circumstances. This is to avoid the unnecessary delay in the trial date that would certainly result if a new attorney were to take over close to the beginning of trial.

Also, some states (i.e., jurisdictions) allow an attorney to hold on to a client's file until the attorney has been paid in full for his or her services. Other jurisdictions do not put such a limitation on a client's choice of representation and require the attorney to forward the file to the client's new attorney once the first attorney receives notification that a new attorney has been retained. However, it is important to remember that you and your child will likely be responsible for any outstanding bills to the existing attorney regardless of whether or not the first attorney forwards the legal file or new counsel has been retained.

Finally, and probably of utmost importance, you and your family must be confident in the legal skills of your child's attorney, and his or her knowledge of the unique characteristics of the entertainment industry, and know that he or she is a zealous advocate on your behalf. There are many great entertainment attorneys for consideration; however, not all have a niche specialty in representing children in entertainment, and these considerations should all be a part of your thought process in selecting an entertainment attorney, given the many special laws and rules that apply specifically to children in entertainment. If you and your family are in doubt as to any of these issues, then it is usually time to look for another attorney who can provide the legal services necessary to ensure a positive outcome for your child and your family.

As discussed in the next chapter, there is an additional, and often overlooked, way to get out of an entertainment contract with a minor.

# CHAPTER 33

## A CHILD'S RIGHT TO DISAFFIRM (CANCEL) A CONTRACT

*When I was 11 [my mom] made me sign a contract and
it said 'I will not ever get a tattoo.' I had to sign my name,
and my sister had to do the same thing.*

—Dakota Fanning

In Chapter 11, we learned that children are different. Nowhere is that more clear than with respect to cancelling contracts.

By law, a minor's promise, whether verbal or in writing, does not alone create any legal duty or obligation. The law has, for many years, permitted minors to simply walk away from their contracts. This is true of a wide array of contracts, not just those related to entertainment. Minors are generally permitted to cancel their contractual obligations and treat them as if the contract never existed in the first place.

The legal term for a minor cancelling (or voiding) a contract is *disaffirmance*. A minor may disaffirm his or her contract, including an entertainment contract, unless certain steps are taken to prevent a child from disaffirming.

> **ROBERT'S TIPS:** The effect and power of disaffirmance is best expressed by use of a little bit of legal jargon. Lawyers and judges often use the Latin phrase void *ab initio* to describe the impact of disaffirming a contract—which simply means the contract is void from the beginning or from its very inception.

Parents of children in the entertainment business, and children old enough to understand the concept, should realize that disaffirmance is a serious act and can have wide-ranging legal implications. Therefore, the act of disaffirming a contract, if done at all, should be done cautiously and only after careful and deliberate contemplation and consideration. If things are falling apart in your relationship with your Talent Agent or Talent Manager, consult with an experienced entertainment lawyer so you can evaluate the long-term practical *and* legal aspects of disaffirmance, including issues of fairness and professional ethics.

## How to Disaffirm a Contract

Under California law, there is no official, formal way to disaffirm a contract by a minor, but there are preferred ways to do so. No magic language is required to make the disaffirmance valid. The key is that the intent to disaffirm the contract's binding force and effect be clear and explicit. However, according to at least one court, *termination* and *disaffirmance* are different and require different action on your part to implement one or the other. Therefore, as a practical matter, anyone disaffirming a contract would be wise ti ensure that the letter or notice disaffirming a contract or transaction is signed by your child and by your lawyer, and that it contains specific language that a court would recognize as showing a clear intent to disaffirm.

## Deadline for Disaffirming a Contract

Under the law, a minor (also legally termed an "infant") is someone who "has not reached full legal age." In most states, a person reaches full legal age at 18 years. Subject to a few important exceptions, a minor can, therefore, disaffirm a contract at any time up through his eighteenth birthday.

The law in California is slightly different. It provides that a minor can disaffirm a contract at any time before his/er eighteenth birthday, "or within a reasonable time afterwards." It's clear that a child can disaffirm a contract before he/she turns eighteen. But what does "or within a reasonable time afterwards" actually mean? It is fairly clear that a minor doesn't lose the right to disaffirm on the day he/she turns eighteen, but how much more time does one have?

Unfortunately, courts in California have not yet defined the phrase "or within a reasonable time afterwards." We did, however, come close to finding out how a California court would have decided the issue in the context of a case involving a famous celebrity. While you may have never heard of disaffirmance, you probably do recognize the name Vanessa Hudgens; she is one of the stars of the Walt Disney *High School Musical* Motion Picture franchise.

So what does Vanessa Hudgens have to

do with disaffirmance? Plenty.

On September 17, 2007, Vanessa's then entertainment attorney, Brian L. Schall, sued the young actress in the Los Angeles Superior Court for breach of written contract and other related legal theories, claiming she owed him $150,000 in back commissions for his legal work on her movie, songwriting, and recording career.

The written attorney-talent contract was a rather straightforward "attorney-client letter agreement" frequently used in the entertainment industry between actors and attorneys. The contract had an effective starting date of October 1, 2005, when Vanessa was just sixteen years old. Only the attorney and Vanessa, who was unaccompanied during the meeting, signed the contract. Under the contract, Vanessa, a minor at the time, agreed to pay him five percent of the gross compensation earned and/or paid while he represented her. In addition, she also agreed to pay him five percent of the gross compensation earned and/or paid after the contract terminated, if such compensation was earned by Vanessa while the law firm represented her or within twelve months after the termination. Vanessa's attorney admitted in the lawsuit papers that she had paid "some, but not all the money owed to him" and claimed a balance due of $150,000.

After Vanessa was sued, she hired a new attorney, who immediately forwarded a letter dated September 28, 2007, directed to the original attorney, and signed by Vanessa, providing "notice of disaffirmance" of the written contract for legal services.

In explaining why she was disaffirming the contract with her former attorney, Vanessa stated, among other things, that he was fired because she was growing weary of his representation, calling his services "below professional standards, resulting in a breakdown of their relationship."

Vanessa was sixteen years old when she entered into the contract with Mr. Schall. But, and this is the key, she was eighteen years and nine months old when she sent the letter of disaffirmance. Surely Vanessa Hudgens had a strong argument that she disaffirmed her contract in a timely fashion.

Interestingly, in an unrelated case, a United States Court of Appeals in Kentucky, interpreting California law, found that an attempt to disaffirm a contract made seventeen months after the minor had reached the age of majority (i.e., after turning eighteen years old) was "untimely"—simply too late under the facts of that case. Would a California court agree? We don't know just yet. Although the facts of every case are different and must be evaluated independently, we might, at least until we hear otherwise from a California court, presume that the phrase means something more than a few days after a minor reaches his or her majority and something less than seventeen months afterwards.

My professional opinion is that, given the circumstances of Vanessa's case, her notice of disaffirmance at eighteen years and nine months was probably well within her rights, and well within the definition of before her eighteenth birthday "or within a reasonable time afterwards." But we don't know for sure. The lawsuit between Vanessa Hudgens and Mr. Schall was settled before a judge decided whether Vanessa's letter was timely or not. Since the California courts have yet to directly consider what the phrase means, and because the judge in Vanessa's case did not give us any guidance, don't assume that it is too late for your child to disaffirm a contract simply because he/she is now older than eighteen.

If your child has already turned eighteen and is considering disaffirming a contract, don't delay—it's possible, if not likely, that he or she may be able to disaffirm that contract for several additional months or more. Contact an experienced entertainment lawyer to help you evaluate the legality, as well as the pros and cons of this decision.

## THE EMANCIPATED MINOR EXCEPTION

Not every minor is entitled to disaffirm a contract. Specifically, in terms of the law, an emancipated child is treated as an adult for most everything other than drinking, driving or getting married. As a result, since adults cannot disaffirm a contract, an emancipated minor may not disaffirm a contract.

> **ROBERT'S FACTS:** Emancipation is a legal term that describes the process of freeing someone from the legal control of another—typically one's parents. Hollywood tabloids will often condescendingly refer to emancipation as "divorcing" one's parents, but such a cynical view is not always justified.

Emancipation is a legal process where, in some states (e.g., California, but not New York), a court can declare a minor, who is at least fourteen years of age (in California), to be an adult before he reaches the age of eighteen. Emancipation requires court approval and, other than in the rarest of circumstances involving physical or financial abuse, parental agreement. With emancipation, a child no longer has to answer to his/ her parents. Equally, it also marks a time when the parents are no longer responsible for their children; they no longer have to provide for their emancipated children, be it financially or even as to basic necessities such as food and shelter. Clearly, emancipation is a serious matter. While emancipated minors possess more freedom than their peers, their legal rights vary from state to state.

Emancipation, however, is often misunderstood as it relates to the entertainment industry. Occasionally, parents and teenagers confuse the issue of being emancipated with *automatically* limiting or minimizing on-set schooling requirements and/or how many hours a young actor may work on set each day. Let's clarify the issue.

What many people do not realize is that California labor regulations are still fully applicable to an emancipated minor, *unless the emancipation document specifically exempts the minor from California Title 8 (CCR § 11750 et seq.).* That is the body of law that sets forth all of the employment rules and regulations, including schooling rules and regulations for a minor working on a TV show or Motion Picture.

Therefore, short of engaging in the difficult and often questionable emancipation process, the only practical way around the requirements for on-set schooling is for your child to pass a high-school-equivalency examination and obtain a certificate of proficiency. The requirements relating to on-set schooling, passing a high-school-equivalency examination, and obtaining a certificate of proficiency are explained in California *Labor Code* §1391.2 and *Education Code* §48412.

Some minors file for emancipation from their parents because they are trying to gain control over their careers or finances (well-known examples include Hollywood celebrities such as Michelle Williams, Jena Malone, Drew Barrymore, Jaime Pressly, and Macaulay Culkin).

But when parents and producers encourage emancipation, it is for different reasons—they are usually looking to skirt the strict California law which requires work permits, limits on-set working hours, required on-set education, and/or the presence of a Studio Teacher, and the application for emancipation seeks an exemption from *Title 8* requirements. They use emancipation as a tool, so they can employ the minor for the same hours and the same work and duties as an adult. While producers are usually looking to maximize screen time, parents who seek to emancipate are hoping to simplify life or to gain a competitive edge on other kids in the business.

Although it is an uncommon process, emancipation can be a successful tool for those who carefully evaluate all of its consequences. For example, during the filming of the movie Crush, Alicia Silverstone, then sixteen, became an emancipated minor—reportedly in order to get around child labor laws which would have interfered with her working hours. She was a dedicated actress from early on, and the film caught the attention of Aerosmith, who hired her to appear in a string of their music videos. The first of them, Cryin', was voted the #1 video of all time on MTV, making Silverstone a definite hit with the MTV crowd. It also served as an impetus for her future success. That said, emancipation was not designed to deal with these specific operational issues. Rather, it is a far-reaching concept, which involves changing the child's legal status and treating him/her as an adult. Although not impossible to obtain, successful emancipation is a formal and, in some respects, an extreme process.

In fact, emancipation is addressed in this chapter only because it affects a minor's ability to enter into legal contracts. In short, if a child is emancipated, he/she can enter into a contract (and do a litany of other adult-permissible activities) without his/her parents' permission. Unfortunately for the child, with this status also comes the reality that the child bears many of the consequences of being an adult, including that he or she can be sued in his or her own name.

As is discussed in the next two chapters, there are circumstances beyond emancipation that more commonly limit or prevent a child from disaffirming an entertainment contract.

# CHAPTER 34

## PREVENTING DISAFFIRMANCE BY SEEKING COURT APPROVAL

*Obedience of the law is demanded, not asked as a favor.*

—Theodore Roosevelt

Short of emancipation, discussed in the previous chapter, the only way to overcome a child's right to disaffirm a contract is to obtain court approval of that contract.

In California, *Family Code* §6751 establishes a somewhat underutilized procedure for obtaining such approval. Under that section, "[a] contract, otherwise valid . . . entered into during minority, *cannot be disaffirmed* . . . if the contract has been approved by the superior court . . . ."

The idea behind court approval is that the judge will act as the guardian of the child's interests with respect to that contract. Unlike the Talent Agent, production company, or studio that contracts with the child, the judge has no financial stake or other interest in the contract. Thus, in theory, the judge is in a good position to evaluate whether it is appropriate to give up the child's right to disaffirm a particular contract.

The preliminary question that must be answered relates to who, among your representatives, can seek court approval.

Under *California Family Code* § 6750, et seq., production company (e.g., studios, networks, producers) contracts can be, and regularly are, submitted to the Los Angeles Superior Court for approval. The California Talent Agency Act likewise has a provision under *Labor Code* § 1700.37 which authorizes Talent Agents and agencies to submit their talent contracts with minors for approval by the court. While agents do not utilize this process as often as the studios, networks and production companies, we are seeing more and more filings by agents in recent years.

As for attorneys, *Family Code* § 6602 states that a "contract for attorney's fees for services in litigation, made by or on behalf of a minor, is void, unless the contract is approved by the court," which likewise gives the court the power to approve the attorney-actor/client agreements.

Talent Managers, however, because they are unregulated, are not

## CASE STUDY

*My overwhelming experience is that most people, including parents, Talent Agents, Talent Managers, attorneys, judges, and even appellate justices unfamiliar with this area of law greatly underestimate the sheer, broad power of disaffirmance for contracts not approved by the Court. For a long time, I wondered why. It was only recently that I concluded that because most law is not "black or white" nor without exception, since the power of disaffirmance is so clear and absolute, it is often resisted and difficult to accept. The Court, in Berg v. Traylor, helped solidify the point by saying it this way: "The law shields minors from their lack of judgment and experience and, under certain conditions, vests in them the right to disaffirm their contracts. Although in many instances such disaffirmance may be a hardship upon those who deal with an infant, the right to avoid his contracts is conferred by law upon a minor 'for his protection against his own improvidence and the designs of others.' It is the policy of the law to protect a minor against himself and his indiscretions and immaturity as well as against the machinations of other people and to discourage adults from contracting with an infant. Any loss occasioned by the disaffirmance of a minor's contract might have been avoided by declining to enter into the contract."*

authorized to submit a petition for approval of their management contracts with the children they represent. California does not currently have a statute authorizing the approval of management contracts, and the court will not consider the request, called a "Petition for Approval of Minors Contract."

In summary, while Talent Agents, production companies, studios, networks and attorneys can utilize the court approval process to prevent a minor from disaffirming the contracts entered between them, Talent Managers cannot prevent a minor from disaffirming the contract they enter with them. This is not likely to change for Talent Managers until there are state regulations in place addressing the issue.

Generally speaking, you and your child should cooperate fully if you sign a contract that you want for your child and your Talent Agent or the production company later presents it for court approval. There are, however, important practical considerations regarding who has the duty to seek court approval and who will pay the costs and attorney's fees for that process. Specifically, you should cooperate in the process, but don't agree to pay for it.

The issue of payment generally won't come up in the context of a contract between your child and a production company or studio. They routinely take on the responsibility for obtaining court approval of contracts with minors. They also pay for the costs and attorney's fees incurred in obtaining that approval.

The issue of payment is, therefore, most likely to come up in connection with contracts between your child and Talent Agents. In short, there is little justification for your agreeing to pay for the costs of obtaining court approval. As of January 1, 2014, the court-filing fee in Los Angeles County was $435, and that does not include the costs for an attorney to prepare and file the petition and related court documents.

In summary, do not agree to any contract that gives your representative the right to recover their attorneys' fees for obtaining court approval for a contract with your child. After all, the process of seeking court approval primarily benefits Talent Agents, production companies, and studios by removing your child's right to disaffirm your contract with them. If they want court approval, it's only fair that they should pay for it.

The information in the next chapter explains an alternative protection from disaffirmance used by *both* Talent Managers and Talent Agents.

# CHAPTER 35

## "INSURANCE" AGAINST DISAFFIRMANCE: SEEKING PARENTAL AGREEMENT

*Education is when you read the fine print;*
*experience is what you get when you don't.*

—Pete Seeger

Talent Managers, Talent Agents, and others who contract with entertainment children are understandably concerned about disaffirmance or other ways that the child can terminate a contract and/or avoid paying them. The "Parental Agreement" is their back-up plan. If, for one reason or another, someone who contracts with your child doesn't get paid by your child, that person will want someone else to pay him. Who is that someone else? You—the parent.

In California, a parent does not have the right to enter into contracts, including an entertainment contract, on behalf of his or her child. Yes, you read that correctly. I understand that parents try to negotiate and sign contracts for their children all the time—but doing so is not legally binding on your child.

California *Family Code* §6701 says it this way; "A minor cannot... give a delegation of power...." This simply means that a child cannot grant the power to enter a contract (with a few designated exceptions) to anyone, even his/her own parents, without the permission of the court. And, by the way, while we as parents can take away the cookies, TV watching "rights," and even the car keys, we can't just take this power, nor do we automatically have this right. I know this is a shock to most parents, but this is the law in California.

Let me explain. A parent can enter contracts for a child related to medical and healthcare issues and generally even sign a liability release related to a school program for his/her child because the law imposes on parents a duty to provide for the *health* and *welfare* of the child—but that's about it. Essentially, a parent can only enter a contract for his/her child for things related to necessities for the child and his or her family. While people struggle with this all the time, precedent-setting cases in California completely support this principle. Many parents mistakenly believe they can sign virtually any contract "for their child." They can't.

Parents can, however, enter into a contract *that obligates them* to pay a Talent Agent or Talent Manager. That is why an increasing percentage of talent agency and talent management contracts include language that attempts to bind the parents to the minor's contract. This language is, among other things, entitled *Parental Agreement* or *Disaffirmance*.

Parental Agreements come in all shapes and sizes. They're sometimes just a paragraph embedded within a longer contract, and sometimes they are written as separate addenda to the talent management or talent agency contract between the child and the manager and/or agent. Either way, they're getting more sophisticated than ever before, which generally means they're longer. However, in their simplest form they usually boil down to something like this:

> *Parent agrees to take no action which might influence Artist to breach, disaffirm, terminate, void or invalidate this Agreement or any part thereof. Parent separately and independently further agrees that Parent is personally liable for all commissions and costs advanced due Manager under this Agreement, regardless of any action to disaffirm or otherwise invalidate this Agreement taken by Artist. Regardless of any action Artist may take in the future, independently or otherwise, to disaffirm this Agreement, whether successful or not, such action will not cancel, terminate, void or avoid Parent's obligations under this Agreement. Parent further agrees that all services performed by Manager are equally beneficial to both Artist and Parent.*

I have no doubts that provisions like this will be the subject of future litigation and new laws. That's because a parent has a duty to protect his/her children, which raises the question of whether a mere contract provision that the parent will "take no action which might influence Artist to breach, disaffirm, or terminate" can remove that long-established legal duty. That said, as of the writing of this book, all parents who sign a Parental Agreement should consider it binding.

More importantly, for now at least, keep in mind that this type of paragraph does not change or take away your child's right to disaffirm and void the contract. Your child's rights are independent, and remain theirs. However, a Parental Agreement may, and likely will, independently obligate the parent who signs it *to pay* for the manager's (or agent's) commission and costs due under the contract with the child. In other words, a parent who agrees to be bound by the terms of the contract will likely be on the hook for unpaid commissions and expenses, even if his/her child disaffirms the contract.

Parental agreements or disaffirmance provisions can have an enormous impact on parents' obligations under the Talent Manager's or agent's contract with their children. All parents must realize these provisions are really the Talent Manager's or agent's insurance plan if they have problems enforcing their contract with the child for whatever reason—"and that back up plan is for action against you, the parent."

# SUMMARY OF PART VI

## GETTING OUT OF ENTERTAINMENT CONTRACTS

Now that you know how contract termination generally works, let's summarize how it specifically applies to different kinds of entertainment contracts. Contracts with Talent Agents, Talent Managers, and production companies and studios are subject to different rules.

### TERMINATING A CONTRACT WITH A TALENT AGENT

- Talent Agents, at least in California, must be licensed by the Labor Commissioner of the State.

- Talent Agents and agencies are regulated by state law in California, under the Talent Agencies Act, *Labor Code §§ 1700 et seq.*

- The California State Labor Commissioner must approve all forms of contract used by Talent Agents and talent agencies.

- The form of contract of a SAG-AFTRA-franchised Talent Agent includes a built-in opt-out provision. The form of an ATA talent agency contract may or may not, depending on its terms, include an opt-out provision. For additional information on the differences between SAG-AFTRA and ATA talent agreements, see Chapter 3.

- The initial term of a SAG-AFTRA-franchised Talent Agent contract is one year. The initial term of an ATA talent agency contract can be one year or longer, depending on what is negotiated and, thus, the termination date depends on the terms of those contracts. For additional information on the differences between SAG-AFTRA and ATA talent agreements, see Chapter 3.

- Talent Agents can insert renewal provisions in their talent contracts.

- If a Talent Agent materially breaches his obligations under his contract with you, you may be able to terminate the contract.

- Your child may disaffirm a Talent Agent contract until he/she is age eighteen or a reasonable time thereafter, unless the contract has been approved by the Court.

- The Talent Agencies Act permits a Talent Agent or agency to seek court approval of its contract with a minor and, if that approval is granted, this prevents your child from disaffirming the contract.

- Talent Agents may ask you to pay for the costs and attorney's fees related to seeking court approval, but you should reject this request.

- As a backup, Talent Agents can and do request parental agreements, which can obligate the parent to pay for unpaid agency commissions and expenses in the event the child disaffirms the contract.

## TERMINATING A CONTRACT WITH A TALENT MANAGER

- Talent Managers are not licensed in California.

- If you want to include an opt-out provision in a contract with a Talent Manager, you generally need to negotiate for it.

- The initial term of a Talent Manager contract is typically three years and can include automatic renewal provisions.

- If a Talent Manager materially breaches his obligations under his contract with you, you may be able to terminate the contract.

- Your child may disaffirm a talent management contract until he/she is age eighteen or for a reasonable time thereafter.

- Unlike a Talent Agent contract, in California, a Talent Manager cannot seek court approval as a way to prevent a minor from disaffirming a contract. The California Courts do not authorize Talent Managers the right to seek court approval, because California statutes do not expressly provide for this right. Talent Managers in California, therefore, can't prevent a child from disaffirming his/her contract.

- Talent Managers may not know that they can't seek court approval for their contracts. In my experience, most are unaware of this limitation.

- As a backup, Talent Managers can, and frequently do, insert parental agreements which obligate the parent or parents to pay for any unpaid commissions or expenses in the event the child disaffirms the contract.

## Terminating A Contract with Production Companies and Studios

The process of negotiating with and terminating contracts with production companies and studios unfolds differently than contracts with Talent Agents or Talent Managers. When Talent Agents and Talent Managers negotiate with you and your child, one of their concerns is whether or not they will be timely and fully paid. However, when you enter into a contract with a production company or studio, the money flows in the opposite direction; they pay your child. As a result, many of the factors relating to terminating a contract operate very differently.

- The length of a production company contract varies tremendously. It can be as short as one day, for a Day Player appearance on a television series or when shooting a commercial spot, to six and one-half years, for a contract to appear as a Series Regular on TV.

- If a studio or production company materially breaches its obligations under a contract with you, you may be able to terminate the contract.

- Your child may disaffirm a production or studio contract until he/she is age eighteen, or for a reasonable time thereafter, unless the contract has been approved by the Court.

- Large studios and even smaller independent production companies routinely seek court approval of contracts with minors. Walt Disney Pictures, for example, reportedly seeks court approval of all contracts with minors above the role of Background Actors and Actresses.

- Large studios and production companies will almost always pay for the costs and attorney's fees of seeking court approval. Their contracts will not ask you to pay for such costs.

- Because large studios and production companies almost always seek and obtain court approval for their contracts, your child will not be able to disaffirm such contracts.

- In the rare event that a television or movie studio does not have a contract approved by the court, your child may disaffirm that contract until he/she is age eighteen, or for a reasonable time thereafter.

## Termination: A Complex Decision

Just because you can terminate a contract doesn't mean that you should. Termination is an important decision that has potentially far-reaching consequences for you and your child. When you terminate a contract (especially before its ending date), the other side may not be happy with you. At a minimum, this may involve the exchange of unpleasant letters, emails, or phone calls. But there is also a chance that the relationship between you and your child's Talent Agent, Talent Manager, production company, or studio will involve a lawsuit or some other more formal process for resolving disputes. Lawsuits involving entertainment children are relatively rare. But you can't fully protect yourself, your child, or your family without understanding how disputes are handled in the entertainment industry.

That's the subject of Part VII.

# PART VII

*Dispute Resolution*

# Part VII

## Dispute Resolution

It's natural for people to avoid thinking about what they will do if their relationships—personal and business—might end. This is especially true when you first start working with someone who offers hope and promise to your child by handing you a contract to sign, and you are excited about the possibility of what you can achieve together.

But if you want to protect yourself, your family and your entertainment child, you should know how Hollywood resolves disputes. Once the dispute begins—and entertainment industry disputes often revolve around money and who controls it—the language in the contract that describes how disputes will be resolved becomes paramount.

Part VII outlines the four most common methods of resolving disputes in Hollywood and describes what happened to Craig and MeShiel when Craig's Talent Manager, Sharyn Berg, sued them for money she believed she was entitled to receive under the talent management contract that MeShiel had signed.

The Chapters in Part VII are:

- Craig Makes it Big and Sharyn Berg Sues
- Four Ways Entertainment Industry Disputes Are Resolved
- MeShiel and Craig are Forced to Arbitration
- Craig and MeShiel go to Court
- Craig and MeShiel Appeal

# CHAPTER 36

## CRAIG HITS IT BIG AND SHARYN BERG SUES

*Fame you'll be famous, as famous as can be*
*With everyone watching you win on TV,*
*Except when they don't because sometimes they won't.*

—Dr. Seuss, *Oh, the Places You'll Go!*

After the second season of *Malcolm in the Middle* wrapped, Craig received a significant increase in pay. His new contract with Fox paid him more than $15,000 per episode. He was now a Series Regular on a bona fide hit TV show. He was appearing more often than anyone other than the stars of the show (Frankie Muniz, Jane Kaczmarek, and Bryan Cranston), who appeared in every episode. Craig was appearing regularly—nine episodes during the third season (November 2001–May 2002), nine episodes during the fourth season (November 2002–May 2003), and eight episodes during the fifth season (November 2003–May 2004).

Craig's financial outlook improved even further during that fifth season. That's because on March 21, 2004, the 100th episode of *Malcolm in the Middle* aired, and that meant that the show was eligible to go into syndication. With that, Craig and the other Series Regulars were going to receive increased royalties, which could be considerable.

You can imagine that Sharyn Berg looked at this situation with a certain amount of frustration and dismay. After all, she felt she had done what Talent Managers are supposed to do, and what they are paid to do—help in the overall development of their clients' career. Craig was working regularly, but since MeShiel's September 2001 letter, Sharyn Berg wasn't getting paid. Based on her 15% commission and Craig's episodic rate of $15,000, Sharyn believed that she was owed at least $2,250 for every episode that Craig worked. She also felt that the contract that MeShiel had signed back in 1999 entitled her to a cut of any income Craig would receive from the show's syndication.

Finally, during the first half of 2004, Sharyn Berg filed a lawsuit against Craig and MeShiel in the trial court for Los Angeles County. The lawsuit alleged that Craig and MeShiel had violated the 1999 Talent

Management contract and sought payment of all the money that was allegedly owed to her as a commission for the episodes and residual income from reruns, including syndication payments Craig had already received, and the payments he would receive in the future, as well as repayment of a relatively small amount of money that Sharyn had lent MeShiel.

For MeShiel, the lawsuit came as a complete surprise. In her mind, years had passed and the matter was well behind them, and long forgotten. MeShiel had heard absolutely nothing from Sharyn Berg for more than two years. MeShiel found out about the lawsuit from her husband, who was "served" with the lawsuit papers. (The person being sued must be notified of the lawsuit in some official way. Formal service of a lawsuit does just that.)

MeShiel didn't know it at the time, but she was about to embark on a journey that would expose her and her young son to enormous emotional and economic burdens and years of litigation utilizing almost all of the ways in which entertainment-related disputes are resolved in Hollywood.

# CHAPTER 37

## FOUR WAYS ENTERTAINMENT INDUSTRY DISPUTES ARE RESOLVED

*Talk is overrated when it comes to settling disputes.*

—Tom Cruise

We all like to believe that our business relationships will remain harmonious and never sour. Unfortunately, for a variety of reasons, parents and children on the one hand, and Talent Managers, Talent Agents and productions companies on the other, sometimes no longer see eye-to-eye, resulting in unforeseen disputes. When that happens, the language of the contract that describes how disputes will be handled becomes the focal point. It describes and oftentimes limits what happens next, including the legal process and procedures, and maybe most important, what state law applies to the dispute.

That is how it should be. One of the reasons why people negotiate contracts and reduce them to writing is so that everyone involved in the contract understands, up front, the terms on which the relationship will proceed. As such, the section of the contract that is often entitled "Dispute Resolution" describes how disagreements about the contract will be handled, where the dispute will be resolved, who will be at the helm of, and deciding the outcome of, the proceedings, and other circumstances related to resolving the dispute.

> **ROBERT'S TIP:** The Dispute Resolution language of entertainment contracts is important for another reason. It is well understood by industry insiders that certain ways of resolving disputes tend to be more favorable to one side than another. Thus, the language relating to Dispute Resolution can have a direct impact on who will likely have an advantage, even before the resolution process begins.

If you, as a parent, want to protect yourself and your entertainment child, you need to know about the four ways in which entertainment industry disagreements are resolved.

- A hearing before the California Labor Commisioner

- A lawsuit resulting in a trial before a judge or a jury
- Court-Ordered or Private Voluntary Mediation
- Binding Arbitration

## HEARING BEFORE THE CALIFORNIA LABOR COMMISSIONER

If your contract with a Talent Agent or Talent Manager is governed by California law, and your contract does not require submitting your case to arbitration (discussed below), the case must in most circumstances first be submitted to the California Labor Commissioner, an administrative governmental body. Until recently, the Commissioner had exclusive jurisdiction over all disputes between Artists, and any Person, (which includes a Talent Agent or Talent Manager), who violates or is charged with violation of the *Talent Agents Act*.

Most people in the industry familiar with the process hold the opinion that the Labor Commissioner is certainly *artist-friendly* when it comes to resolving disputes between an artist and his or her representative. Indeed, rulings over the years support this belief.

The California Labor Commissioner will hear disputes between actors and Talent Agents and those between actors and Talent Managers which involve, among other things, a claim the manager violated the *Talent Agencies Act* by illegally procuring employment for the actor. The decision of the California Labor Commissioner in these matters is not binding, and if either side is unhappy with the result, he or she may seek a new trial (the official Latin phrase for this is *Trial de Novo*) in the Superior Court.

However, the Commissioner's "exclusive" powers to hear and decide these disputes were undermined by a recent United States Supreme Court case, *Preston v. Ferrer*, which held that the California Labor Commissioner no longer has the exclusive right to hear disputes involving alleged procurement violations. *Preston v. Ferrer* involved a dispute between television celebrity "Judge Alex" and his Talent Manager. The Supreme Court found that if the parties agree to have the matter resolved by way of arbitration, that such an agreement is effective and the matter does not have to be, in such circumstances, submitted to the California Labor Commissioner, but rather must proceed under the agreed upon arbitration provision in the contract between the talent and his or her representative. Thus, for example, if a contract with a Talent Manager contains language indicating that disputes will be handled through arbitration, the dispute won't go to the California Labor Commissioner, but if a talent management contract designates the Labor Commissioner or is silent about how disputes shall be resolved, the dispute will first be submitted to the Labor Commissioner. After it goes there, the dispute can go through the traditional lawsuit process, if the parties are unhappy with the Commissioner's decision.

## LAWSUIT LEADING TO A TRIAL BY JUDGE OR JURY

When most people picture what a lawsuit looks like, they see a crowded courtroom with a judge and a jury. This is a scene that has been shown thousands of times on TV and in Motion Pictures, because it is the most historic and traditional forum for resolving disputes in America.

From the perspective of entertainment industry insiders, there are distinct advantages and disadvantages to having juries resolve entertainment industry disputes. The biggest advantage is that the court system has established procedures for handling every aspect of a dispute. For example, when someone files a lawsuit, each party gains the power to collect a wide array of information related to the dispute. The technical term for the process of collecting information related to a lawsuit is known as "formal discovery."

In the court system, each side has very broad discovery rights. Specifically, each party can compel people and organizations to answer questions verbally, under oath, in person (depositions), and in writing (interrogatories), and provide documents (both as hard copies and in electronic form). The people who work for the court system, such as judges, clerks, and court reporters, are experienced. Likewise, the court system has a process in place for finding and selecting jurors. The jurors have a civic duty and legal obligation to participate, and the parties to the case don't have to directly pay for the salaries or expenses of any of the people who work in the court system, as those costs are paid by all of our tax dollars. The court system is particularly well suited to resolving a dispute when you need to access information and obtain documents and sworn statements that you otherwise wouldn't be able to obtain.

### Concerns About the Court System

Studios, production companies, Talent Agents, Talent Managers, and the actors and actresses themselves, however, have differing approaches to resolving disputes, including the extent to which they want to file lawsuits. Many feel that the traditional court system is too slow and expensive, while others have concerns that it is too visible and unpredictable. Let's look at each of these concerns in turn.

*Too Slow:* It is well known that the court system is a time-consuming process. Recent statewide budget and related personnel (judges, court personnel, etc.) cuts have magnified the problem and further slowed the process. That's why it can now take years for a traditional lawsuit to wind its way through the court system. Depending on what side of the dispute you are on, this can be considered an advantage or a disadvantage, but most would prefer a faster alternative.

*Too Expensive:* Because of the extensive discovery rights that litigants have in the court system, many entertainment insiders feel that too much time and money is spent on turning over documents and providing other information that ultimately isn't important to the dispute. They feel that the discovery process in the court system is overkill.

The cost of lawyers is also an enormous concern. In most entertainment disputes that involve disagreements about a contract, lawyers charge by the hour. These fees can add up quickly. Moreover, the traditional rule in this country is that each side pays its own lawyers.

**ROBERT'S TIP:** In the United States, if you want to have the losing side pay the winner, that language generally needs to be added to the contract. Look for language that says that "the prevailing party" is entitled to recover reasonable attorneys' fees and costs.

*Too Visible:* The court system is a public institution. As a result, with few exceptions, what happens in that system is open to the public. If you file a lawsuit or one is filed against you or your child, the media and bloggers may know about it within hours. Likewise, the public and media have the right to attend court hearings.

You and many people in the entertainment industry might prefer a more private alternative. For example, just because you are having a contract dispute with your Talent Agent or Talent Manager doesn't mean you want the details of that dispute to be visible to the press and the public.

*Too Unpredictable:* Although judges are generally experienced, most do not have a lot of entertainment-industry experience. Many judges are more familiar with criminal law or general civil law than Entertainment Law. For people who work in the entertainment industry, that relative lack of experience can create unpredictability.

The greatest source of unpredictability in the traditional court system, however, is not the judges. Hands down, it's the jury. People who work in studios, production companies, and as Talent Agents and Talent Managers are understandably nervous about having people who know nothing about their industry resolving their disputes. They feel that letting a jury decide is a gamble and, to a large extent, this is a legitimate concern.

The fact that people in the entertainment industry have certain concerns about the court system does not mean that they don't use it. They do. In fact, if a particular written contract is silent about how disputes will be resolved, that means that all the parties to that contract will use the traditional court system (except for disputes in California that first go to the Labor Commissioner). This is also true if there is no written contract and there is a dispute about a verbal agreement.

In our current environment, filing a lawsuit that might end in a jury trial now tends to be the fallback process for resolving most disputes. That is because, as described below, the concerns that people have expressed about the court system have led many in the entertainment industry to use alternative methods to resolve disputes.

## Court-Ordered and Voluntary Private Mediation

### Court-Ordered Mediation

Although a lawsuit filed in court can end in a jury trial, it almost never does. More than 95% of lawsuits settle or leave the court system well before they get to trial. Judges, of course, know this. They are also very protective of court time. Judges don't want to go through the process of calling up and selecting a jury only to find out that the case could have been settled.

Consequently, all judges and court systems now require people who are involved in a lawsuit to go through some form of mediation or a settlement conference before they are allowed to proceed to trial.

Mediation is a method of non-binding dispute resolution involving a neutral third party who works to help the disputing parties reach a mutually agreeable solution. The mediator can't force either party to settle; that's what makes it non-binding.

During mediation, the people who are having the dispute are typically brought together in one setting. The mediator carefully evaluates all sides of the dispute and tries to help the parties reach common ground. Mediation can involve lawyers, but doesn't have to. In a court-ordered mediation, the mediator will report back to the judge, and let him or her know whether or not the case settled. The details of what happened in the mediation, however, are confidential and not disclosed to the judge. In a court-ordered mediation, the mediator either volunteers his or her time or is paid by the court, but either way it is free to the parties.

### Voluntary Private Mediation

Mediation is certainly the most cost-effective method of dispute resolution and is very efficient. If successful, it can help all parties avoid the enormous time, expense and emotional heartache of litigation. With the exception of the court-ordered mediation described above, or a mediation that is required by a contract you signed, you cannot be forced to submit a dispute to mediation. Mediation is voluntary and only works if both sides of the dispute agree to it. Mediation is an effective process often used to resolve everything from very simple to highly complex disputes.

As a result, many times parties to a dispute elect to hold a Voluntary Private Mediation, which has the benefit of giving you the chance to choose someone who has the specific experience that would help resolve a particular dispute. Voluntary Private Mediation of entertainment disputes is often mediated by someone who has lots of entertainment-industry experience and is a skilled professional mediator. Unlike court-ordered mediation, the costs of the mediator are generally shared equally by the parties.

Given its potential benefits, you should at least consider mediating a dispute with a Talent Agent, Talent Manager, or other entertainment industry insider. I have had great success in Voluntary Private Mediation over the years. A good entertainment lawyer can help you identify and select mediators that might be right for you, and a good industry insider acting as a paid mediator can get to the heart of a problem with ease and efficiency and find common ground for resolving even the most contentious disputes.

## BINDING ARBITRATION

Since the Supreme Court's decision in *Preston v. Ferrer*, an increasing percentage of entertainment contracts include language requiring disputes to be handled through arbitration. In the absence of such contractual language, you cannot be forced to have your dispute resolved through arbitration. Arbitration and mediation, often confused, are very different methods for resolving disputes. Arbitration, by definition, is a binding process, whereas mediation (discussed above) is not. Despite this, arbitration is often redundantly referred to as Binding Arbitration. In other words, with few exceptions, the decision of the arbitrator is final.

Arbitration clauses are not only found in many traditional Talent Agency and Talent Management Agreements. Indeed, SAG's Agency Regulations and Contracts (aka Rule 16[g]) and Legacy AFTRA's Agency Regulations and Contracts (aka Rule 12-C) each contain a provision requiring that disputes and controversies between an agent and a SAG-AFTRA member arising out of, or in connection with, any agency contract must be heard in arbitration before the American Arbitration Association (AAA). I have argued, on behalf of actors and actresses, that California procedural laws provide exceptions to these provisions, but those at the helm of SAG-AFTRA, whom I admire and respect, do not believe any such exceptions exist. Thus, challenging the issue is multifaceted and complex, and since such a discussion is beyond the scope of this book, it will be the subject of an independent article in the near future. In short, review all contracts carefully and have them reviewed by an entertainment attorney.

Arbitration is a well-accepted and often-used procedure to resolve disputes of all kinds. In short, arbitration is akin to a "mini-trial" before either a retired judge or an experienced arbitrator—typically an attorney with experience in the particular area of dispute (i.e., the entertainment industry). Arbitration has become so widely accepted as an alternative to a traditional trial in a court of law, that private organizations exist which specialize in providing all of the necessary elements to have a case arbitrated, including a long list of experienced arbitrators from which to choose and facilities where the hearings are held.

Several well-known organizations offering these services are JAMS (Judicial Arbitration and Mediation Services), AAA (American Arbitration Association), ADR (Alternate Dispute Resolution), and Judicate West. The advantages of arbitration are: (1) the parties can schedule the hearing at mutually convenient times, something not available in a court of law, (2) the hearing is generally much shorter in length, and (3) although still potentially expensive, the entire process is usually much more affordable than a full-blown court trial before a judge and a jury. One of the disadvantages is the fact that the decision of the arbitrator, called the Award of Arbitration, is binding and, with few exceptions (e.g., arbitrator misconduct), there is no right to appeal.

Another significant advantage of arbitration over a court proceeding is that it is a private dispute-resolutions process, which means that nothing that is said or occurs becomes part of a public record, and that can include the very fact that there is a dispute. This is often critically important in the entertainment industry where issues of reputation, confidentiality and privacy are so important.

## WHAT TO LOOK FOR IN AN ENTERTAINMENT CONTRACT REGARDING DISPUTE RESOLUTION

There are numerous variations on how the issue of dispute resolution may be presented in an entertainment contract. For example, a recent contract drafted by the lawyers at NBC for a TV Series Regular performer, who was a minor, called for the application of California law utilizing JAMS arbitration. In contrast, contracts from Disney and FOX drafted at the about the same time didn't require disputes to be resolved by arbitration, but rather by a traditional trial court proceeding in California, applying California law.

You will also see a variety of approaches in contracts with Talent Agents and Talent Managers, with some going the arbitration route and others leaving the option for hearings before the California Labor Commissioner and a follow-up lawsuit in state court, if needed. What follows are two sample provisions you might see in a management contract. The first also allows the prevailing party to recover attorneys' fees, but only if the parties previously tried to resolve the dispute through mediation.

> ***Mediation Required—Attorney's Fees****: Any dispute arising from or related to this agreement shall first, before any other formal action is taken, be mediated before a mutually selected, single mediator. Mediation fees and costs related to mediation, if any, shall be divided equally among the adverse sides.*
>
> *Any prevailing party in any administrative, arbitration and/or court proceeding arising from or relating to this Agreement shall*

*be entitled to an award of its reasonable attorney's fees and costs of litigation. However, if a prevailing party fails to first attempt to resolve the matter through mediation, or refuses to mediate within a reasonable time after a request has been made, then that party shall not be entitled to recover its attorney's fees as set forth elsewhere in the Agreement.*

The example above encourages pre-litigation dispute resolution by mediation and does not state how the case will be resolved if the mediation is unsuccessful. In this scenario, either the Labor Commissioner or Trial Court would decide the case, since there's no reference to arbitration in the agreement. Also note if one party is unreasonable and refuses to mediate, they lose their right to recover attorney's fees even if they ultimately win, even though the contract otherwise provides that the prevailing party can recover attorney's fees.

Here's another sample paragraph you might see in the talent management contract, either following the above paragraph, or standing on its own:

***Dispute Resolved in Arbitration—Attorney's Fees:** The agreed and appropriate forum for enforcement of this Agreement is arbitration in Los Angeles, California, pursuant to Commercial Rules of the American Arbitration Association. Each party shall be entitled to conduct limited discovery, pursuant to California Code of Civil Procedure Sections 1283.05 and 1283.1, consisting of no more than two depositions, one set of document demands, one set of no more than twenty-five interrogatories, and service of as many business records subpoenas as the arbitrator may permit, on good cause shown. The arbitrator may allow further discovery only upon a finding of good cause shown by the requesting party. The prevailing party shall be entitled to an award of reasonable attorney's fees and costs of litigation. In accordance with California Labor Code §1700.45, the California Labor Commissioner shall be given reasonable notice of the time and place of all arbitration hearings, and the Labor Commissioner and/or its authorized representative shall have the right to attend all arbitration hearings.*

*By agreeing to arbitrate any disputes, each party is waiving their right to a jury trial.*

This second example requires arbitration before a specifically designated organization offering those services. It also allows the parties to engage in "limited discovery." This means either side can engage in a variety of court-authorized formal investigation procedures, such as depositions (a verbal interrogation in the presence of a court reporter) and interrogatories (written questions). These conditions help both sides prepare for the arbitration hearing; however, they do increase the cost of the process. This provision also requires the losing party to pay the attorneys' fees and costs of litigation for the prevailing party.

## WHICH PROCESS IS BEST FOR YOU?

Unfortunately, there's no single answer to that important question, other than to say that the issue should be carefully and seriously contemplated.

If we polled a dozen judges, mediators and attorneys, we would get a variety of answers—but one common theme would keep coming to the forefront: each would want to know more about the particular case before selecting the best process. This is because the best process depends upon factors such as:

- How many parties are involved

- Whether the case is simple or complex

- Whether there are complex legal issues to be resolved that could confuse people who are not legally trained, in which case you might want a judge to decide them and the right to an appeal

- What type of issues are in dispute (Does the case involve enforcing the rights of the parties, money and compensation, or both)?

- Where the parties reside

Unfortunately, when you're signing the contract, many of these factors are unknown. We can, however, use the following generalizations to decide what dispute-resolution process or mix of processes is best in a particular circumstance.

When taken seriously, the nonbinding Voluntary Private Mediation process should be a prerequisite to any of the remaining alternate dispute resolution formats mentioned above. Of all of the processes, mediation is the simplest and least expensive and, in my experience, has a very high success rate, even in the most vigorously disputed and contentious matters.

When it comes to the binding process, Arbitration is a risky alternative to a court trial because instead of getting a judge and a jury of twelve peers to decide the case, you get one arbitrator who acts as the judge *and* jury. If this single selection happens to be a bad one for you, the entire arbitration can become a difficult and frustrating uphill battle. That said, many talent agency and talent management contracts now contain a provision requiring arbitration rather than a trial by jury, so you'll likely end up agreeing to utilizing that process. On a positive note, arbitration is generally more affordable and less time-consuming than a trial by jury. Additionally, to avoid the problem mentioned

**CASE STUDY**

*A great mediator will often, almost miraculously, find a way to assist disputing parties in reaching an amicable settlement even when it seems impossible. Not long ago, I was counsel for a party brought to mediation in which the two parties loathed and despised each other and had each drawn a "line in the sand." They were well over a million dollars apart when the mediation began at 9:00 AM. The mediation persisted into the night. At 10:30 PM, with the parties still more than a half a million dollars apart, everyone packed up to leave. The mediator insisted that he be given a few more minutes to solve the case, and requested permission to meet privately with the two parties, followed by a private meeting with counsel. Forty-five minutes later, the mediator was able to announce that a settlement had been reached. This is a testament to the fact that a great mediator can resolve almost any "impossible case" and save thousands of dollars in legal fees and costs. As you can imagine, I have used this mediator again.*

above, an experienced attorney has ways to help assure that an acceptable arbitrator is selected.

In cases involving complex legal issues or a significant amount of money, it is often beneficial to provide for a three-person arbitration panel, rather than a single arbitrator. That not only reduces the possibility of an unreasonable decision; it allows the inclusion of experts on the panel who could be important in some cases. For example, the lead arbitrator could be an attorney experienced in entertainment matters to rule on objections and other legal matters and the other two arbitrators could include an accountant, for example, if there were complex money distribution problems, or a Talent Agent who might have a different perspective. The downside is that this adds two more arbitrators who will need to be paid, but the amount of money being fought over may very well make that investment worthwhile.

Finally, many talent agencies and Talent Managers use a contract that calls for arbitration by the American Arbitration Association (AAA). This does not seem to be a deliberate choice. Rather, many seem to use contracts that are handed down from their colleagues. Thus, the reference to AAA arbitration becomes self-perpetuating. While many might disagree, I would not recommend the American Arbitration Association as the arbitration or mediation service of choice. The Association's costs and fees are unusually expensive and the process unnecessarily cumbersome. No, I did not have a personal bad experience with the AAA. To the contrary, the few cases I have had before them have been very successful. But I believe that most parents and entertainment children should avoid AAA arbitrations because of their cost.

Now that you have an understanding of the various ways in which entertainment contracts can be resolved, let's turn to a real-life example—the dispute between Sharyn Berg, on the one hand, and MeShiel and Craig on the other.

# CHAPTER 38

## MeShiel and Craig Are Forced to Arbitration

*The jury, passing on the prisoner's life,*
*May in the sworn twelve have a thief or two*
*Guiltier than him they try.*

—William Shakespeare, *Measure for Measure*

The Artist's Manager's Agreement that MeShiel had signed indicated that disputes relating to the contract would be resolved by arbitration according to the rules of the Judicial Arbitration and Mediation Services, Inc. (JAMS). The arbitration was initially scheduled for December 2004.

The months following, leading to the arbitration, were a particularly difficult time for MeShiel. She was pregnant with her third child when her husband, Craig's father, was killed in a car accident. Less than a month later, not surprisingly, MeShiel was hospitalized with pregnancy-related complications. Consequently, the arbitration was postponed for two months.

The half-day arbitration hearing took place in early February of 2005. Sharyn Berg was there along with her attorney, Brad Kane. MeShiel was no longer represented by an attorney. She showed up, accompanied by Craig's agent, Stephen Rice, who was there for emotional support and to request additional time so MeShiel could retain counsel. Craig, who was fourteen at the time, did not attend the arbitration, because MeShiel knew very well that he knew absolutely nothing about the contract he had never seen, into which was entered when he was just ten years old, so she sent him to school, treating it as a normal school day.

At the arbitration, MeShiel and the Talent Agent begged the arbitrator for an extension of time so she and Craig could retain an attorney. She explained about the tragic, sudden death of her husband and her hospitalization for complications in pregnancy. The arbitrator denied the request and expected MeShiel to defend the case against Berg and her counsel.

Sharyn Berg's lawyer argued that Berg was entitled to her commission under the contract for money that Craig had been paid since September 2001, for interest, and for her commission on his estimated future earnings.

In addition, the lawyer also sought payment for about $3,000 that Sharyn Berg had lent MeShiel, plus interest. MeShiel did not deny the existence of the loan or its amount, or that she had sent the September 2011 letter, which terminated Sharyn Berg. The arbitrator noted that MeShiel "presented herself as a pleasant person." The entire arbitration lasted several hours. MeShiel did the best she could, but she was no match for Sharyn Berg and her lawyer, Brad Kane.

The arbitrator issued his written decision a week later. Despite the kind words that the arbitrator had for MeShiel, his decision was disastrous for her and Craig. Craig and MeShiel were ordered to pay Sharyn Berg more than $150,000 in commissions (plus accrued interest) for money that Craig had already been paid (under his per-episode contract and for reruns and syndication). The arbitrator also ordered MeShiel to pay back the loan and accrued interest. This totaled an additional $5,100.

Most importantly, the arbitrator decided that Berg was entitled to commissions on six years of Craig's future syndication payments. The arbitrator concluded that six years was a reasonable period of time for a hit show like *Malcolm in the Middle* to be in syndication. For this six-year period, the arbitrator decided that Berg was entitled to $405,000 in future projected earnings. Given that Berg's commission was fifteen percent, this was the equivalent of predicting that Craig's payments from syndication and future per-episode appearances would total $2.7 million over six years, or $450,000 per year. Because the original Talent Management Agreement included language granting attorney's fees to the winner of the arbitration, MeShiel was also ordered to pay for Sharyn Berg's lawyer—an additional $13,000.

As a result, the arbitrator's decision meant that MeShiel and Craig were ordered to pay Sharyn Berg the total sum of more than $578,000.

The arbitrator's decision regarding Craig was perhaps even more shocking. Despite the fact that Craig was only fourteen, and that he had gone to school on the day of the arbitration as his mother had told him to do, the arbitrator held Craig's failure to show up at the arbitration against him. Specifically, the arbitrator entered a "default judgment" against Craig. In this context, "default judgment" means that someone who fails to show up in court or at a similar proceeding is essentially deemed to have waived all of his rights. Here, the arbitrator decided that Craig's failure to attend the arbitration justified treating him as if he didn't object to what Berg and her lawyer were saying or trying to do at the arbitration. Yes, you read that right; the arbitrator entered a default judgment against an unrepresented child!

There is, however, a difference between winning an arbitration award and actually getting paid. This is true for many aspects of law. There are a variety of processes that exist that convert an arbitration award into actual dollars. In particular, the Award of Arbitration requires going to court and getting a judge to sign off on it, in order to enter it as a formal judgment.

That is what Sharyn Berg's lawyer did next. He went to court to see if he could convert the arbitrator's decision to a judgment—and in turn, actual dollars for his client. That is where the next phase of MeShiel and Craig's legal saga took place—in the Superior Court in downtown Los Angeles.

# CHAPTER 39

### MESHIEL AND CRAIG GO TO COURT

*Justice denied anywhere diminishes justice everywhere.*

—Martin Luther King, Jr.

Six months after the arbitration, on a Saturday afternoon in August 2005, I received a phone call. It was Stephen Rice. He asked if I could help one of his clients with a legal problem. He explained that this client had lost a case in which an arbitrator awarded more than $500,000 against the client, in favor of a Talent Manager. I'd heard such stories before, but this one was unique, because this client was a minor—in fact, only a ten-year-old child when he put his trust in and signed a contract with the Talent Manager. While Stephen knew very well this was a serious issue, to me it sounded like much more than just a problem—it sounded like a disaster.

To compound matters, there was some built-in urgency. The Los Angeles Supreme Court trial judge in the case was literally days away from entering the arbitration award, all $578,000 of it, as a final court judgment collectable against both the child and his mother. I immediately requested a copy of the file, which was sent over. Unfortunately, it was in complete disarray, with important documents clearly missing. Despite that, I could well discern what had happened, and worse yet, what was about to happen.

I knew that if there was any hope at all, I had to quickly look into the details of the case to see if I could prevent Craig and MeShiel's nightmare from becoming a complete catastrophe. I agreed to meet with the child's mother the very next day—a Sunday morning. That's when I first met MeShiel. We met together, along with Darryl Dickey, a lawyer I have known and respected for twenty-five years. Darryl is as calm and unruffled as can be. Nothing fazes him. MeShiel was understandably distraught and tearful, wondering how things could have gone so wrong. She was very clear that she lacked the funds to hire a lawyer. We talked for several hours, and I realized with certainty that the results were so wrong and simply had to be made right, so I accepted the case.

Despite the seeming hopelessness of the circumstances and history of tortured litigation, I firmly believed that the arbitration decision was wrong. More than that, I believed that it might not be too late to reverse that decision, if we could just get someone in the court system to listen.

Next, I sent Berg's attorney a "Notice of Disaffirmance of Arbitration Award by Minor" and I filed the original Notice with the court. The Notice essentially disaffirmed (cancelled) the talent management agreement, including the arbitration award. In the Notice, I asserted that the act of disaffirmance voided the contract Berg had entered with Craig Traylor, a minor, and also the arbitration award against the minor. I certainly hoped it did. Additionally, I requested that the court refrain from entering the Award of Arbitrator as a formal judgment, pending documents that I would be filing within two weeks.

Within that time period, I filed and scheduled the matter on the court's calendar for a hearing on a "Petition to Vacate Arbitration Award," which was accompanied by an exhaustive legal brief. This was my first appearance in this case. On behalf of MeShiel and Craig, I argued that: (1) the arbitration award and ruling were wrong—legally unsound and unsupported by the evidence, (2) Craig was a minor with whom an adult cannot legally contract without court approval, (3) this contract was voidable—in fact void *ab initio,* (4) the judge should disregard and void the arbitration award, and (5) the court must, therefore, invalidate all of the proceedings in the case.

The judge completely ignored the arguments and denied my requests, ruling in favor of Berg. Ten days later, in a "Motion for Reconsideration," I requested similar relief from yet another perspective; however, the judge again dismissed the arguments, and frankly, dismissed me as well, saying essentially that my 11th-hour attempt to undo the results of the litigation was "too little, and too late," and he was not going to further consider the matter. A third court appearance fared little better.

After all of that, I was still 100% certain of a few things: (1) the arbitrator was wrong; (2) the trial judge was wrong; (3) the decision was wrong; and (4) the result was wrong. While I was now unsure of our chances of success, I was still 110% sure of one thing—I was the only one, with Darryl Dickey's help, who had any chance to right this wrong.

The next step was clear—we had to, as lawyers say, "take the case up" to the California Court of Appeals, and so we would.

# CHAPTER 40

## CRAIG AND MESHIEL APPEAL

*The real glory is being knocked to your knees and then coming back up.*
*That's real glory. That's the essence of it.*

—Coach Vince Lombardi

Contrary to what many people believe, an appellate court does not automatically accept or undo what the trial court did. While those are among the options, they have wide latitude in formulating their ultimate opinion, including whether it should be kept private or formally published so as to become a precedent-setting and wide-reaching decision for all to see. Additionally, unlike in everyday life, appealing a decision of the trial court that you don't like does not mean that someone else will review everything that happened. Thus, for example, where a trial court hears from witnesses and reviews the evidence, the appellate court would not reconvene all of the witnesses and make an independent decision about whether the arbitrator or trial judge was right or wrong. In fact, the appellate court wouldn't hear from any witnesses. An appellate court reviews the written record of the trial court and both the written appellate brief and verbal arguments submitted by the lawyers for each side.

As a result, it is very hard to successfully appeal a decision of an arbitrator or judge by arguing that they got the facts wrong. Nor are appellate courts likely to overturn or overrule a decision because the results seem unfair. Most appeals do not succeed, but the best chance of success requires showing that the judge or arbitrator made a mistake of law. That was the challenge that MeShiel and Craig had before the Court of Appeals. We had to convince at least two of the three appellate justices who would hear the appeal that the arbitrator and the trial judge had made a mistake of law. Specifically, we had to convince them that they applied the wrong law, or did not apply existing law, and in so doing reached the wrong result.

Although MeShiel and Craig's rollercoaster ride through the legal system raised many issues and sub-issues, on appeal we focused on what we felt were two significant mistakes of law made by the arbitrator and the trial judge. First, the judge failed to appoint someone to protect Craig's interests. The technical legal term for such a person is of Latin origin, the guardian *ad litem*. Literally, it means a guardian for a single lawsuit. A guardian *ad litem*, often a lawyer, is someone specifically appointed by the court to appear in a lawsuit on behalf of an incompetent adult or, as in this situation, a child. This is required because a child does not have the legal capacity to represent himself in a lawsuit. Had a guardian *ad litem* been appointed from the beginning of the case, the whole fiasco involving Craig's non-appearance at the arbitration could have easily been avoided. Since one was not appointed, the arbitrator, in my opinion, had a duty to await the appointment before proceeding with the hearing. This way, whether or not Craig was present, someone, the guardian or someone appointed by that person, would have been able to argue on his behalf.

Second, we argued that the arbitrator and the judge misapplied California law with respect to Craig. Specifically, both were wrong when they failed to recognize that, as a minor, Craig had an absolute right to disaffirm the contract. And, because he could void the contract with Sharyn Berg, she lost her right to enforce the terms, including being paid under the contract.

These were the two main arguments we made in our exhaustive and lengthy Opening Brief. Sharyn Berg's lawyer wrote a compelling and likewise exhaustive Opposition Brief, explaining why the arbitrator and the trial judge made the right decision and reached the correct conclusions, and why our arguments were wrong.

During this time, I contacted Duncan Crabtree-Ireland, the head of the legal department and General Counsel of the Screen Actors Guild (SAG) and requested the Guild support our position in the Court of Appeal. The Guild agreed and, in a show of support and solidarity for its members who are children in entertainment, filed an *amicus curiae* appellate brief. A Latin phrase commonly used in the legal profession, *amicus curiae* simply means "a friend of the court" and essentially refers to someone who is not a party to a particular lawsuit but who, along with one of the parties, petitions the court because of a strong interest in the subject matter. The involvement of the Screen Actors Guild was a sign that Craig and MeShiel's case was important to the entertainment industry as a whole.

In the movies and on TV, we often see dramatic courtroom scenes. But what they don't show you on TV and in the movies is that you have to wait a long time before you get your chance to appear before an appellate court and argue your case before the sitting justices of the Court of Appeals. Months after all the written arguments had been submitted, we were finally assigned a day in February, 2007, on which to show up in person and offer oral argument before the panel of justices assigned to our case.

Two years had now passed since the arbitrator had ruled against Craig and MeShiel and eighteen months since I first met MeShiel. During this period, Craig, in particular, went through important changes. Most noticeably, *Malcolm in the Middle,* had gone off the air a few months before. By all accounts, it was a spectacularly successful show—a total of 151 episodes, and Craig appeared in more than a third of them.

Craig was now less than a month from his eighteenth birthday. When he turned eighteen, he would be an adult in the eyes of the law, and this was significant because the funds in his Coogan Trust Account would be released to him. Coogan Accounts are, by law, blocked, so even the child's parents can't access the money. But there are exceptions. One way to get a Coogan Account unblocked is to get an appropriate order from a judge. Despite the pending appeal, the decisions of the arbitrator and the trial judge also meant that those funds could potentially be reached by Sharyn Berg. The Coogan Account included 15% of all the money that Craig had ever earned in Hollywood, beginning when he was six years old. If he lost the appeal, Sharyn Berg would be in a position to take all of it.

That was what was at stake on February 22, 2007, the day on which Brad Kane and I entered the majestic and historic Court of Appeals courthouse, in Pasadena, California. Because we brought forth the appeal, I went first. I knew that the justices had read everything that all of us had written.

I wanted the justices to focus on what Craig and MeShiel's case was all about. As I approached the podium, I carried with me the mountain of court pleadings, briefs, historical precedent-setting cases, statutes and all of the exhibits that had been filed with the court or were the basis of our appeal. The stack of papers was almost two-feet tall. I placed it on the podium to my right. Brad Kane was sitting at a counsel table further to my right. The courtroom was quiet. Behind me in the packed gallery were about fifty people, including a good number of attorneys, other guests and interested onlookers such as the head of SAG's legal department. Sitting high above and before me was the Presiding Justice of the Appellate Court, flanked on both the left and the right by his associate justices—two women. To their right, in addition to the clerk and the courtroom bailiff, was a small group of appellate court research attorneys and the clerks to the three justices. The Presiding Justice gave me permission to proceed:

> *May it please the Court, good morning, counsel, Justices of the Court. My name is Robert Pafundi and, as you know, I am here before you representing a minor, Craig Traylor, a child actor in the entertainment business.*

I then placed my hand on the mountain of court pleadings to my right:

> *We could spend the little time we have together today rehashing the facts of the case and arguing about the statutes and the laws that apply to this dispute. Certainly, tradition would seem to call for it. However, you have already read every detail. And while all of this documentation, and even the appellate briefs that I filed, may give the impression that there are numerous legal issues and sub-issues before you, and legally speaking certainly there are, in reality, this case comes down to how you will, collectively, answer one very simple question. And, when you have the answer to this question, you will also have the answer to how your opinion in this case should be written.*

Silence filled the room. Each tick on the clock seemed like a minute lost to time. One could feel the doubt that comment had just raised in the mind of the Justices. In fact, one could feel what everyone was thinking, but not saying: *one question—you suggest this comes down to one simple question, really?* I broke my own silence:

> *The question is: Who will Protect our Children? The arbitrator refused to do it, the trial judge refused to do it, which means the only real remaining question is . . . will you do it? Will you protect our children?*

I paused as the silence turned to a deep stillness. Attorneys don't challenge appellate justices. Not a sound could be heard until the calm was broken by the sounds of the three justices readjusting themselves upright and forward, focused intently on me, followed by my words: "If you have any questions I will be happy to entertain them."

When the hearing was over, I wasn't sure whether the Justices of the Court of Appeals had heard. Now we waited.

In the weeks following the oral argument, Brad Kane made one last run at the money in Craig's Coogan Trust Account. He and I both knew that MeShiel lacked the money to pay Sharyn Berg. If she were going to collect the hundreds of thousands of dollars that the Arbitrator concluded that she was owed, that money was going to have to come from Craig. Specifically, it would have to come from the funds deposited in Craig's Coogan Trust Account.

I was, therefore, concerned that Craig's money could be gone before the Appellate Court announced its decision or, if there was no decision, before Craig's upcoming eighteenth birthday, immediately thereafter. I, therefore, wrote a letter to the court, copied to Berg's lawyer, expressing my concern and asking them to reach a decision quickly. Again, I wasn't sure whether they would hear and respond in time.

The Justices of the Court of Appeals published their formal written decision two weeks later. The Justices' decision brought mixed news to MeShiel. The Talent Management Agreement that she had signed almost eight years before included language that very specifically obligated her to pay Sharyn Berg if Craig couldn't or didn't pay. The appellate justices decided that this language was clear and valid. This could have been crushing news for MeShiel, but it wasn't. Sharyn Berg and her lawyer knew that there was no way they were going to collect $578,000 or anything close to it from MeShiel.

Thus, the key question was whether Sharyn Berg could enforce the Talent Management contract and the Arbitrator's decision against Craig.

In a unanimous 3-0 *published* decision, the Justices decided that Craig should have had a guardian *ad litem* appointed for his legal protection *and* that he had an absolute right to disaffirm the Talent Management Agreement. Judicial decisions are usually written in a highly analytical, unemotional style. But these Justices made their disappointment with the arbitrator and trial judge clear.

*Where our difficulty lies is in understanding how…the arbitrator and the trial court repeatedly and systematically ignored Craig's interest in this matter.*

The Court found this oversight by the arbitrator and the court *"nothing short of stunning"* and promptly announced a new standard related specifically to children's rights and how entertainment children would forever be protected from that time forward. The court held that:

> *Because we find that Craig had the statutory rights as a minor to disaffirm both the original contract and the arbitration award, we reverse the judgment (of the trial court) against Craig.*

I had asked the Justices to protect our children. They did.

As a result of the Court's decision, Craig's money in his Coogan Trust Account was safe. Because he had disaffirmed his contract, he didn't owe Berg any additional money. The judgment against him for $578,000 was dismissed.

The timing of the judges' appellate decision could not have been coincidental. It was published on the very day Craig Traylor turned eighteen; the money in his Coogan Trust Account was his—and his alone.

Sharyn Berg had few good options at this point. She could pay Brad Kane to try to take her case one last step further and see if the California Supreme Court would overturn the decision of the Appellate Court. However, it is well known that the California Supreme Court only accepts approximately 3% of all cases submitted, and even if it did, Berg and her attorney knew the case now had a miniscule chance of success for them, and it would have been very costly. Instead, a confidential and satisfactory settlement was reached within just days.

Consequently, the Court of Appeals decision became the final, binding decision in the case and the Court's decision to publish its opinion raised it to the status of being a "precedent-setting" decision on issues related to protecting our entertainment children. The formal citation of the case is *Berg v. Traylor* (2007) 148 Cal.App.4th 809, 56 Cal.Rptr.3d 140.

Craig and MeShiel's rollercoaster ride through the legal system had finally ended. They were overjoyed.

# SUMMARY OF PART VII

## DISPUTE RESOLUTION

Most business relationships in the entertainment industry—with Talent Agents, Talent Managers, producers, and studios—progress along nicely and end amicably. But as with all business relationships, some do not. It is therefore important that, as a parent, you understand the primary ways in which disputes are resolved in the entertainment industry.

- If your contract is silent about how disputes will be handled, the dispute can be resolved through a traditional lawsuit.

- A special rule applies to disputes under California law that involve talent management or talent agency contracts. Such disputes, unless submitted to arbitration, are first submitted to the California Labor Commissioner. The Commissioner's decision is not binding or final. If a party is unhappy with the Commissioner's decision, they can initiate a traditional lawsuit.

- Traditional lawsuits provide access to extensive discovery rights—the right to collect sworn statements and relevant documents related to the dispute.

- Because of concerns about the public nature of traditional lawsuits, their costs, and the unpredictable nature of juries, many written contracts in the entertainment industry require that disputes be handled through arbitration.

- Arbitration is a binding process in which the arbitrator sits as judge and jury and has a final say about the dispute. The decision of the arbitrator is generally not made public, and arbitration can be faster and cheaper than a lawsuit. Many talent agency contracts call for arbitrations to be handled by the American Arbitration Association (AAA). In my experience, other dispute-resolution organizations are preferable.

- Voluntary mediation is the cheapest and often fastest way to resolve an entertainment-industry dispute. Unlike the decision of an arbitrator, which is generally final and binding, the mediator's role is to help the parties in a dispute to understand each other better and to see if some compromise can be reached. When taken seriously, voluntary mediation is the best method for resolving disputes. It is often a good idea to participate in a voluntary mediation before trying any other dispute-resolution process.

# EPILOGUE

*In the end, the only thing you really own is your own story.*

—Hugh Jackman, *Australia*

The Court of Appeals decision ended the dispute between Sharyn Berg and Craig and MeShiel, but it also started a series of changes that continue to reverberate throughout the entertainment industry.

In the days following the publication of the Court of Appeals decision, which is referred to as *Berg v. Traylor*, the most widely read entertainment industry publications, *The Hollywood Reporter* and *Daily Variety*, ran stories about it. Over the course of the following weeks and months, and still today, various segments of the entertainment industry were interested in educating themselves about the impact of the decision.

A wide range of entertainment-industry organizations hosted events at which *Berg v. Traylor* was discussed. Brad Kane, Sharyn Berg's lawyer, Toni Casala, the head of *Children in Film*, Anne Henry, co-founder of *BizParentz Foundation*, Paul Petersen, the founder of *A Minor Consideration*, and I discussed the decision and its implications at various events and seminars for other entertainment lawyers, hosted by the Entertainment Section of the *Beverly Hills Bar Association*. Children in Film, one of the leading on-line organizations (ChildrenInFilm.com) dedicated to educating parents of entertainment children, also hosted a seminar of its own, where I was invited to discuss the issues with parents of industry children. Brad Kane and I also spoke at The Screen Actors Guild, which sponsored a large event for parents at their Los Angeles headquarters.

The *Berg v. Traylor* decision has been referred to as a "landmark" case on the subject of protecting Hollywood's children. It has been discussed and cited as legal authority by many attorneys and both state and federal courts across the nation, including, most notably, in litigation in which I was one of the counsels of record representing Caitlin Sanchez in her *Dora the Explorer* lawsuit against MTV Networks (Viacom International dba Nickelodeon), in the U.S. Court of Appeals for the Second Circuit, in New York.

Nowhere, however, was the impact of *Berg v. Traylor* felt more strongly than within the community of Talent Agents and Talent Managers. When Brad Kane and I spoke at a meeting of the Talent Managers Association, it was clear that, for them, the decision was a wake-up call. One of their experienced and highly regarded members had spent time and effort developing an actor's career only to find out that the contract between them was void—and unenforceable by law. Talent Agents and Talent Managers wanted to make sure that something like that didn't happen to them.

The entertainment industry has been working with children and dealing with issues related to children for decades, but *Berg v. Traylor* helped bring more attention to some of the contractual and legal issues involving minors in Hollywood. Industry insiders long ago knew that, to some extent, working with children was different from working with adults, but the differences were now brought to the forefront and clarified. For example, it is widely known that children working on television and movie sets are subject to rules related to the number of hours they can work and that regulations exist related to on-set education requirements. But outside of a few entertainment lawyers, only a small number within Hollywood were aware of how contracting with children and young adults could impact a Talent Manager or Talent Agent relationship, or an entire entertainment project or production.

This all changed after *Berg v. Traylor*. Today, throughout the entertainment industry, especially in California and New York, there is increased consciousness about the legal and financial importance of properly taking care of business and legal affairs when working with minors. This is a good thing—both in the long term and looking forward. It adds another important dimension that makes Hollywood more sensitive to young performers and how we should all be partners in protecting them.

Since *Malcolm in the Middle* stopped production in 2006, young stars have become even more important to the entertainment industry. Productions such as *High School Musical* and the *Harry Potter* movie franchises have become global phenomena, and have generated hundreds of millions, and even billions, of dollars in revenues. Performers such as Miranda Cosgrove, Selena Gomez, and Miley Cyrus have become superstars. These three performers are now older than eighteen, but the pipeline of shows featuring child performers continues. The Disney Channel's *Shake it Up!* features six young stars, and *Good Luck*

*Charlie*, also on the Disney Channel, features a star who is not yet five years old. Given the success of these shows and the importance of young performers in Hollywood, no one within the entertainment industry wants to jeopardize these kinds of productions by making a mistake on a child's contract.

There have been two specific reactions to *Berg v. Traylor*. First, producers, directors, studios, production companies, Talent Agents, and Talent Managers are much more aware of a minor's right to disaffirm a contract that has not been approved by a court. As a result, and with the exception of Talent Managers whose contracts cannot be court-approved, it is much more common for entertainment-industry insiders to obtain court approval of such contracts. That is one lesson that Hollywood learned from what happened to Sharyn Berg—get your contract approved by a court so that it is legally binding on the child actor with whom you will be working.

Second, more Talent Agents and Talent Managers are including language in contracts entered with child performers that require the parents to guarantee the payment of commissions and costs, and to assume financial responsibility for paying the agent or manager if, for some reason, they can't be paid from the child's earnings. Today, with this added language, it is more likely than ever that a Talent Agent or Talent Manager will pursue legal claims against the parents of entertainment children. It is not reasonable to expect that Talent Agents and Talent Managers will walk away from five- and six-figure paydays. That is why parents are now more likely to be seen as the backup plan for being paid.

Therefore, it is more important than ever that parents know what they are signing and with whom they are dealing *before* they or their children sign a contract with a Talent Agent, Talent Manager, production company, studio or network, or any other entertainment contract. Yes, those in the entertainment industry are far more aware of children and contractual issues. This means that you, as a parent, owe it to your children and yourself to become equally educated in all aspects of the industry so as to level the playing field.

That, in short, is why this book was written: so parents and others involved in entertainment can help protect our children on their road to fame.

## WHERE ARE THEY NOW?

Sharyn Berg is still a well-respected Talent Manager operating through

Sharyn Talent Management, in Los Angeles. She continues to develop the careers of actors and actresses, with an emphasis on child stars. In fact, she currently represents Naya Rivera, who plays the role of Santana Lopez on the FOX hit TV show, *Glee.*

Brad Kane, the lawyer who represented Sharyn Berg, and I actually worked together a few years after *Berg v. Traylor* in an effort to help parents and children who had been victims of an entertainment industry scam. In that case, hundreds of parents had paid thousands of dollars each to "an agency" that made bold and unrealistic promises of success and stardom, but did little or no work on behalf of the children and soon closed their offices and moved out of town. Brad and I keep in touch and still see each other from time to time.

Craig Traylor has come a long way since he played Stevie Kenarbin on *Malcolm in the Middle.* The year after the show stopped production, and with the lawsuit and appeal behind him, Craig graduated from high school. Craig has shifted some of his focus to his passion for art. He currently studies art at Chaffey College in Rancho Cucamonga, California. To spice up his formal education, Craig has become a skilled tattoo artist. He is considered an apprentice, and has his own small, private studio.

Craig continues to pursue his television and Film career with the guidance of a new Talent Agent. In 2011, Craig appeared in the movie comedy *Dance Fu*, with Eric Lane and Cedric The Entertainer.

Craig will likely always be remembered for his portrayal of Stevie Kenarbin, a character who was wheelchair-bound and asthmatic, and who wore glasses. Given the power of television, it's not surprising that some people—including very famous people—are surprised when they meet Craig in person. At a recent Coachella Musical Festival in Southern California, Craig met Sir Paul McCartney, who told him "I thought you really were in a wheelchair," and he really meant it. In fact, Craig never has been in a wheelchair, nor is he asthmatic. He is now twenty-three years old, tall, charming, physically fit, and very good-looking. If you look at the cover of this book, you should be able to pick him out.

Best of all, Craig is a fine young man. He did not succumb to the ills of Hollywood, or to the worst fears of some parents about entertainment kids. As with most Hollywood kids, Craig is well-adjusted, with his feet solidly on the ground. In addition to his fabulous personality, he has an optimistic spirit and a strong spiritual base. Whatever goals, dreams, and aspirations he chooses to pursue, I am confident about his bright and wonderful future.

Last, but certainly not least, MeShiel is a special and hard-working woman. She remains the widowed mother of three beautiful children—Craig, her oldest, along with two younger girls—fifteen-year-old BreIna, and seven-year-old Aubre. BreIna has dreams of pursuing a music career. Aubre, a gifted student who was already studying pre-algebra by the second grade, aspires to play the violin. MeShiel also enjoys hosting a weekly Bible Study for young people, ages seventeen to twenty-four, which Craig and some of his close friends attend.

Professionally, through her company, Meme's Talent Management, MeShiel develops the acting careers of a select number of young actors and actresses. She is also producing two Reality TV shows. One is a talk show related to a variety of issues impacting the lives of teenagers and young adults, and the other tracks and highlights the careers of young and up-and-coming music artists. In addition to being one very busy mom, MeShiel is clearly using her life experiences to help others. I wish her nothing but success.

It was my privilege to represent Craig and MeShiel and to be associated with such fine people. Whatever else they may accomplish, they should take pride that, through their hard work and perseverance, Craig achieved great success as an actor. They did what few others have ever managed to do—they stayed true to who they are and, in the process, changed Hollywood for the better.

# ACKNOWLEDGMENTS

This book has been shaped by, and could not have happened without, the help of many people.

Let me begin by offering my deepest gratitude to Hollywood Legend Talent Agent Mary Grady. This is the woman who not only changed all of Hollywood by how passionately she represented and watched over its children from the moment she founded MGA, The Mary Grady Talent Agency, (Hollywood's original children's talent agency), in 1959, but also dramatically changed my life as well. Mary, although I attempt to do so here, it is difficult to describe how you forever transformed my life by entrusting your historic agency to me in 2000, and in doing so, gave me my "first big break" in The World of Entertainment. I can only hope that my work in representing and protecting children in entertainment honors your legacy in some small way. From one Italiano to another, *Grazie Mary, Grazie, Grazie!!*

I next wish to thank Gideon Grunfeld, to whom I am truly indebted for his incredible insight and creativity that molded an early draft of this book through its many revisions. Your vision and guidance measure among the most influential contributions in getting the version of *Safe Stardom* that follows this page published. I sincerely thank you for all that you did in helping bring this book to fruition and for helping me find my voice as an author.

With deep gratitude I also thank my publisher, Dunham Books, and more so, its founder, the amazing David Dunham, for taking a chance on me, a first-time book author, and for demonstrating incredible patience and professionalism.

My special thanks to Darryl Dickey, who patiently and determinedly co-counseled with me on the appellate briefs in the underlying case of *Berg v. Traylor*, which inspired me, and acted as the foundation for this work, as did he. My gratitude for Darryl's enthusiasm in reviewing this manuscript *twice* for technical and legal accuracy cannot be overstated. You are a great friend, and although I will try to do so here, I cannot thank you enough.

My sincere appreciation to Karen Rinehardt who tirelessly proofread, edited, and offered great insights on an early version of this manuscript, and who helped make *Safe Stardom* into something, which will hopefully be enjoyable for parents everywhere.

My warmest thanks go to Donna Kozik, founder of *Write and Publish a Book in a Weekend*. When I could only see writing a book as a daunting task, it was you who motivated me to "just start writing," so let all of your students know that without your inspiration this book would never have been started, and therefore never have been written.

I first met Gary Schank during the summer between 7th and 8th grade when he, his brother Roy, and I crossed paths while riding our bicycles on Long Island, New York. Who knew then, that now, years later, I would turn to you to read and comment on the manuscript of my first book. You are a great and loyal friend, and I thank you for volunteering for the task and making *Safe Stardom* that much more readable to families everywhere.

To Dana Gilbert and Alison Wilber, I am blessed to have met you and grateful for all you have done for me in getting the final manuscript ready for delivery to my publisher. When I just couldn't write another word or re-read a chapter *one last time* you were both there for me—graciously pushing and nudging me along. I thank you both and will be forever grateful.

Thank you, Alice Sullivan and Alexandra Williams, for your expertise and research in finding the many great quotations used in the final manuscript of *Safe Stardom*, and further to Alice for her insight and brilliance.

I want to let the world know that every author needs an Agnes Gaertner to review his manuscript. Agnes is a brilliant English teacher who patiently read and repaired every sentence. You are a genius!

I also give great thanks and appreciation to Toni Casala, the founder of *Children in Film*, and Paul Petersen, the founder of *A Minor Consideration*, who are my colleagues in the entertainment industry and whose insights and expertise have greatly enriched this book and my life.

One of the fun things about being a lawyer, especially an entertainment lawyer, is that you, too, are constantly entertained, and in the process learn from your gifted and creative clients. Some are actors and actresses, others Talent Agents and Talent Managers, and still others producers and directors. From wherever they come, each brings a novel set of facts and an interesting personality from which both practical and legal issues are explored. I am grateful to all of you for allowing me the opportunity to represent you and learn from you. I hope I have helped some of you along your journey as you pursue your dreams.

To all of you, I am deeply grateful.

# NOTES

## Chapter 3—The Different Types of Talent Agents

You can learn more about which Talent Agents are SAG-AFTA-franchised by visiting its offices in California, or by visiting its online website at www.sagaftra.org.

You can learn more about the ATA and all that it offers by visiting its online website at www.agentassociation.com.

For a detailed chart comparing Rule 16(g) Protections and ATA General Service Agreements, as presented by Agency Relations at the Screen Actors Guild, go to: www.sag.org/your-relationship-with-your-agent.

## Chapter 4—Avoiding Scams

The full text of the Fee-Related Talent Services Act can be found in California Labor Code 1701 through 1704.3. The law is also sometimes referred to as the "Krekorian Talent Scam Prevention Act of 2009," after the author of the law, Paul Krekorian, who, at the time, was an Assistant Majority Leader of the California State Assembly.

Los Angeles Deputy City Attorney Mark Lambert collected evidence related to some of the most egregious scams perpetuated against actors and their families. He became one of the driving forces behind the law.

The Fee-Related Talent Services Act was widely supported in the entertainment industry by the likes of the Walt Disney Company, the Motion Picture Association of America (MPAA), and the American Federation of Television and Radio Artists (AFTRA). The Screen Actors Guild (SAG), even co-sponsored the law behind the efforts of SAG's National Director and Senior Counsel for Agency Relations, Zino Macaluso, who had first-hand knowledge of the scams.

The Los Angeles District Attorney's Office, which prosecutes criminal violations of the Krekorian Talent Scam Prevention Act of 2009, can be reached at (213) 978-8070.

## Chapter 22—Hollywood Labor Unions and Actor's Pay

SAG publishes a 36-page "Young Performers Handbook," which can be downloaded without charge from the SAG Young Performers Website, at http://youngperformers.sag.org/home.

Today, SAG-AFTRA's national office headquarters are located at 5757 Wilshire Boulevard, Los Angeles, California 90036. You can, therefore, learn more about SAG-AFTRA and all that it does by visiting its offices in California, or by visiting its online website at www.sagaftra.org

## Chapter 23—What Do Actors Earn In TV and Film?

For more detailed information on SAG minimum compensation rates for television and feature Films, for all categories of acting and all variations of programming, one can review the entire 2009 SAG Basic Agreement and Television Agreement, along with the related 2011 Memoranda, which are easily accessible on the SAG-AFTRA website, and available to anyone interested in visiting the site. For more detailed information on SAG Minimum Compensation Rates for Television Commercials, as well as the fairly complex Residual Income Compensation Schedules for Network TV, Cable TV, Internet Commercials, and more, one can review the Commercial Rate Sheets on the same website.

### Chapter 24—Health Insurance and Other Benefits

If you are interested in learning more about the full array of union benefits, visit: http://www.sagph.org/html/bthw1.htm for SAG benefits; and http://www.aftra.com/member_benefits.htm for AFTRA benefits.

### Chapter 28—Hollywood Children and the Paparazzi

The comparison of paparazzi being like "flies on a dead carcass" can be found at: http://blogging.la/2009/08/11/the-paparazzi-pursuit/.

For the reference to the speculation about Michael Jackson's last photo, see the *Paparazzi Reach Their Zenith Capturing Michael Jackson's Death*, The Paparazzi Reform Initiative Blog (July 7, 2009).

The complete text of Ms. Follet's article can be found at 84 S. Cal. L. Rev. 201 (November 2010). See: http://lawweb.usc.edu/why/students/orgs/lawreview/documents/SCalLRev84_1Follett.pdf.

# INDEX